This Book Belongs To

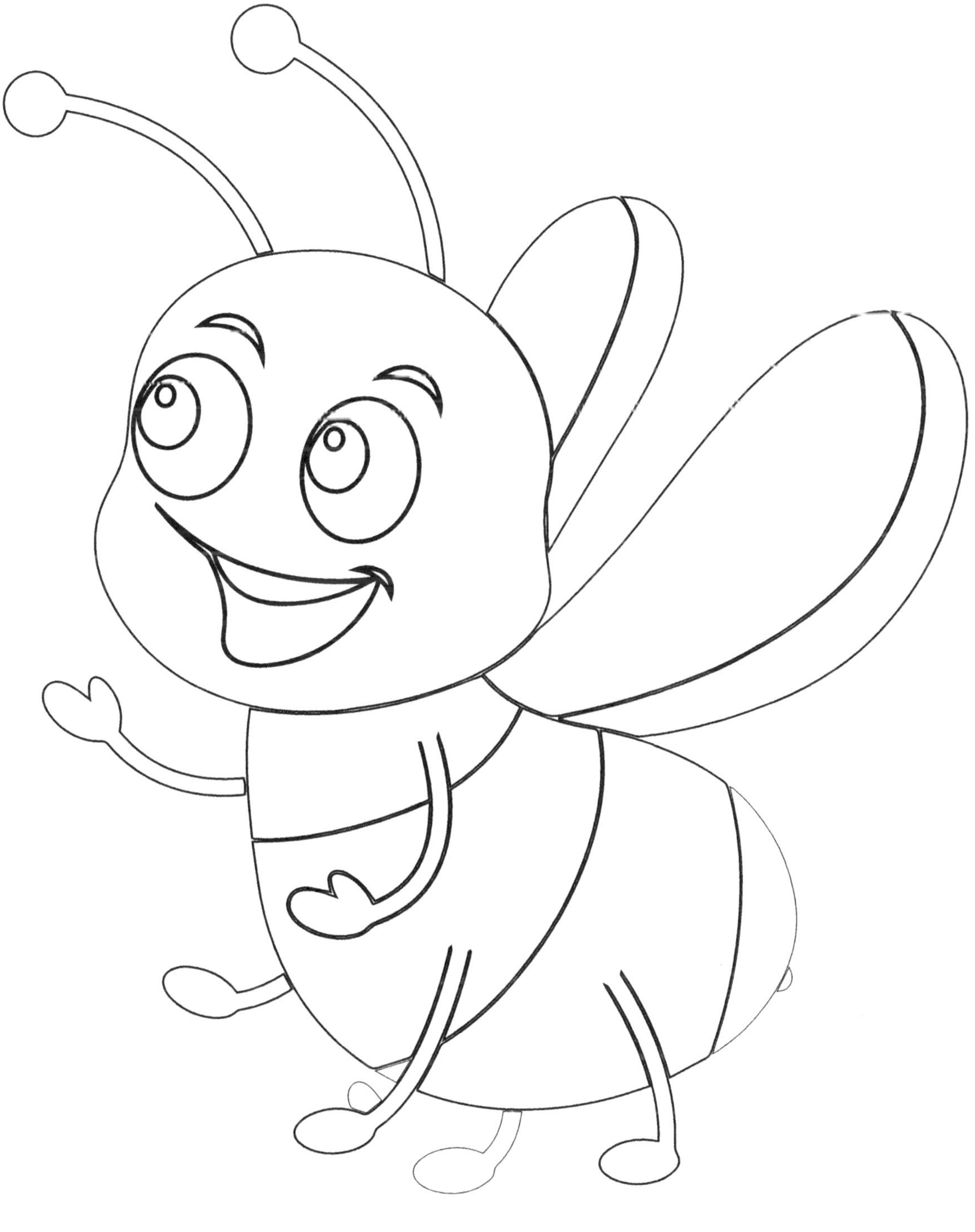

COLOR TEST

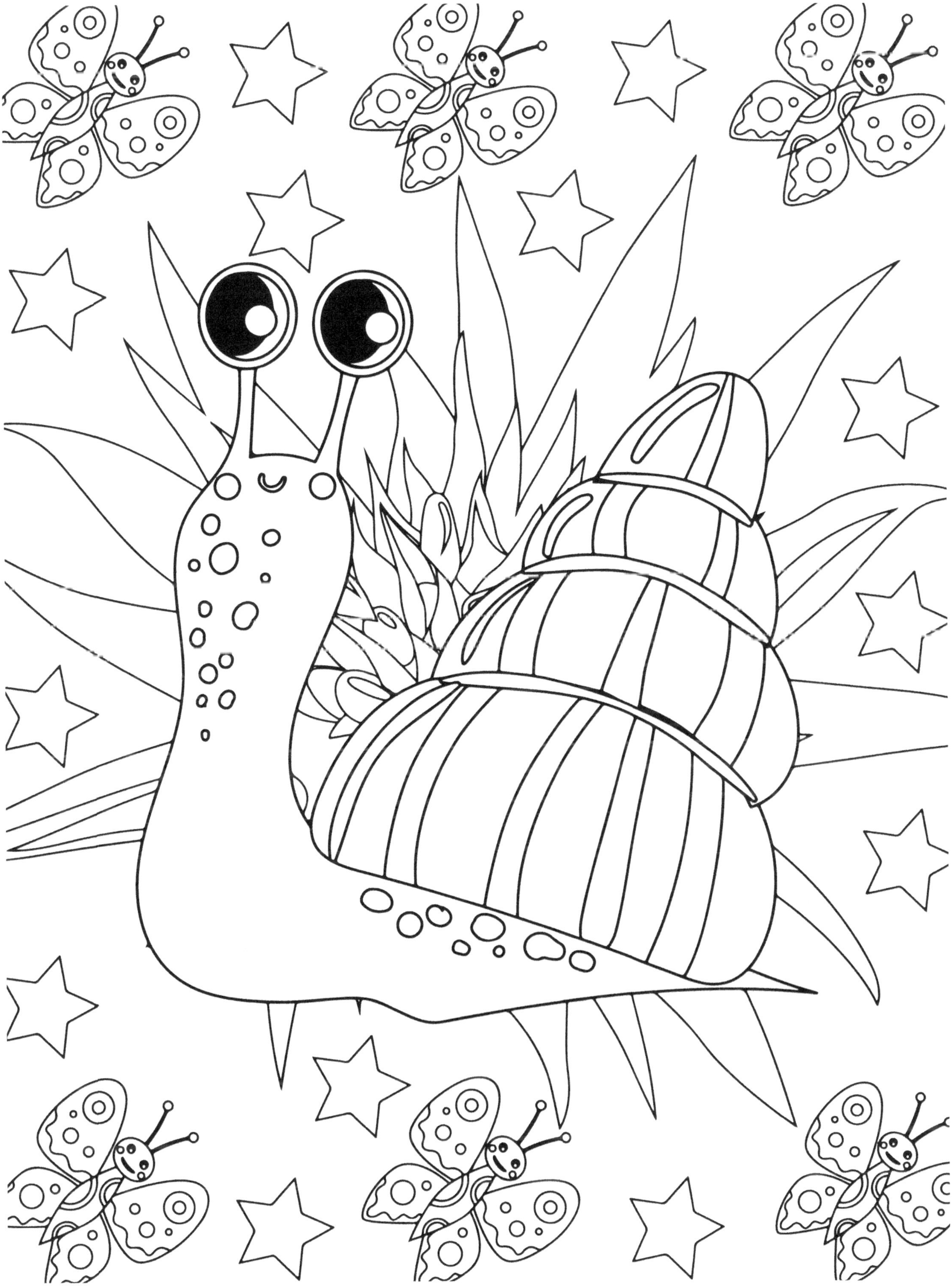

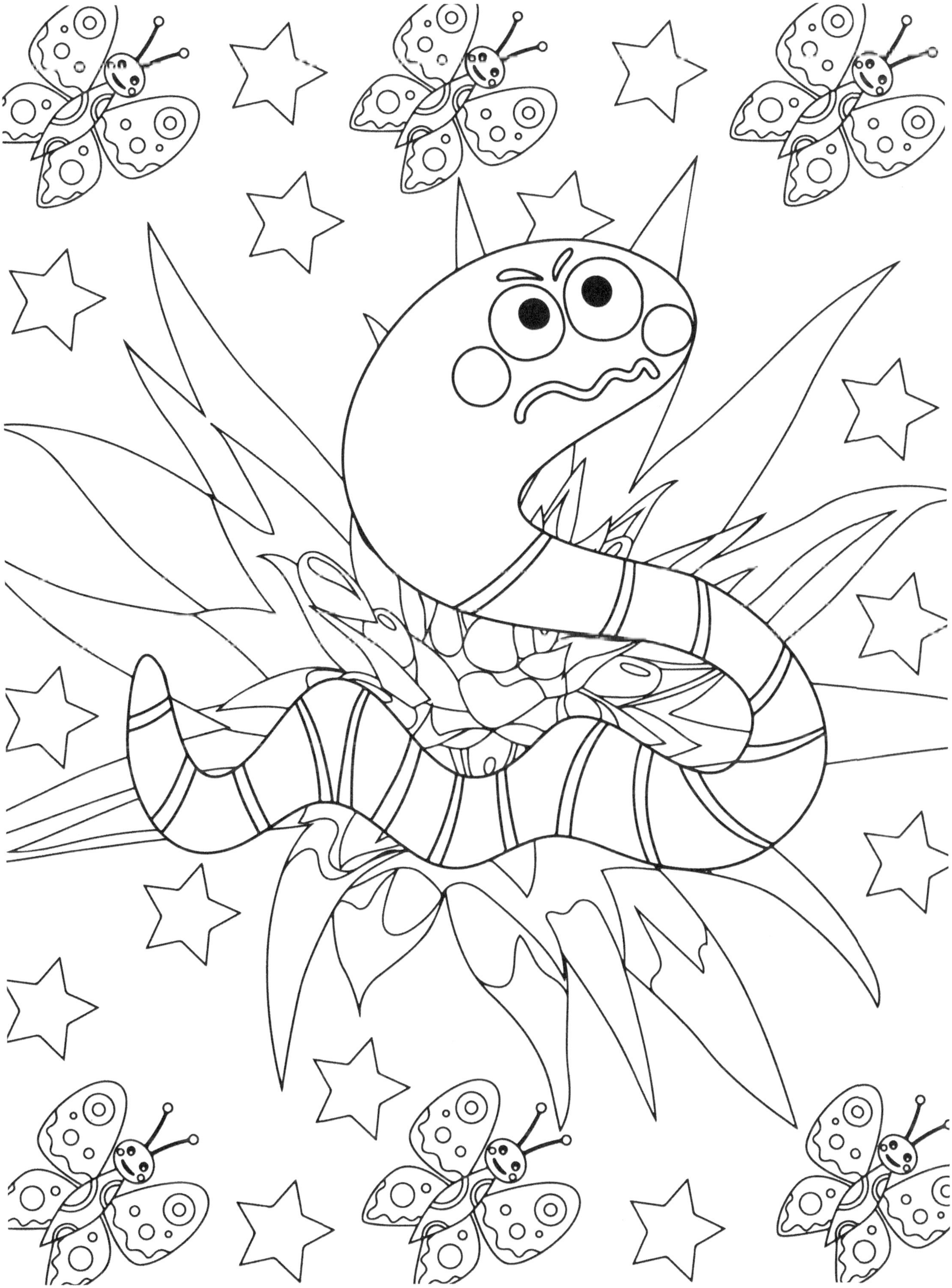

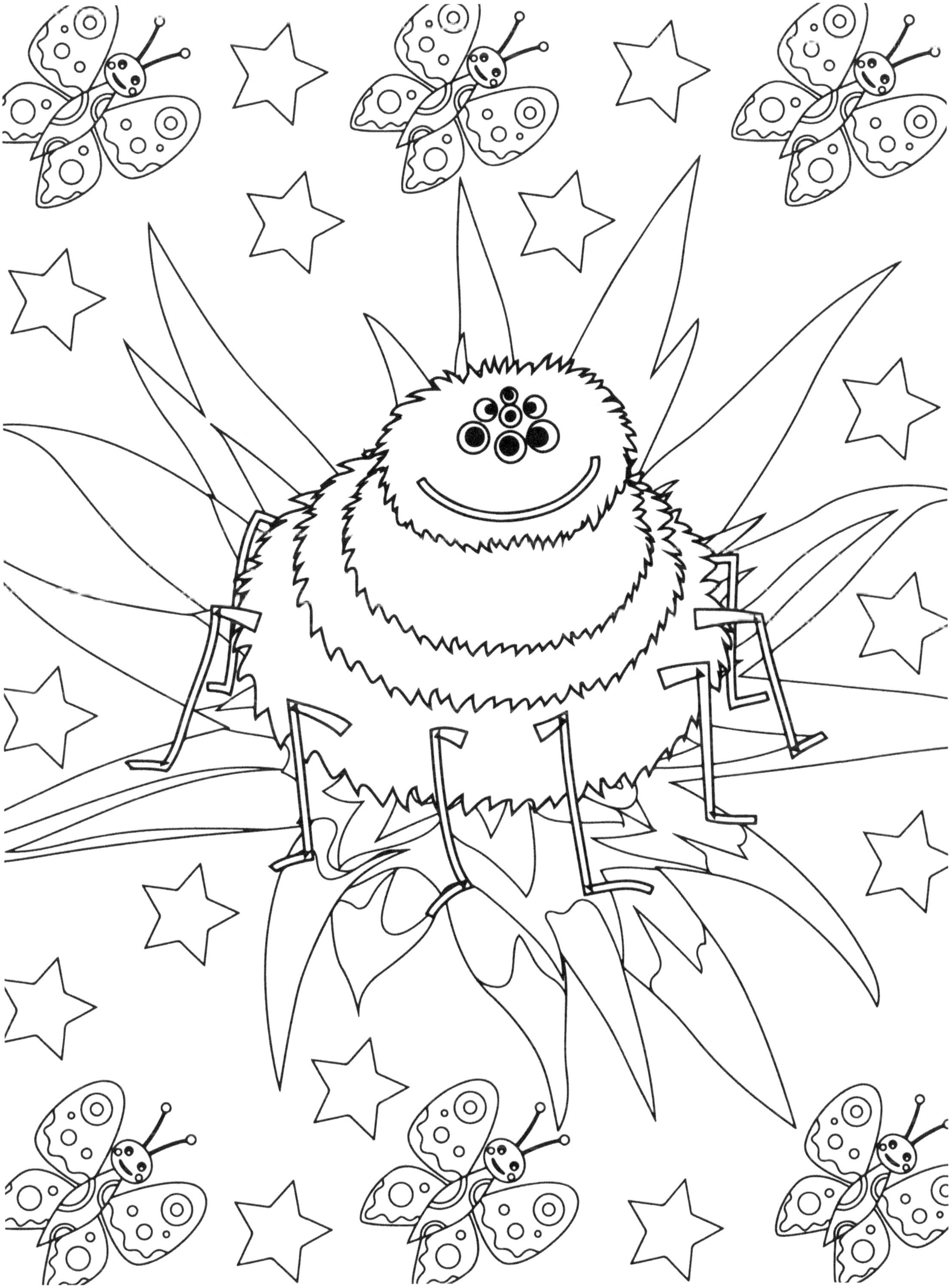

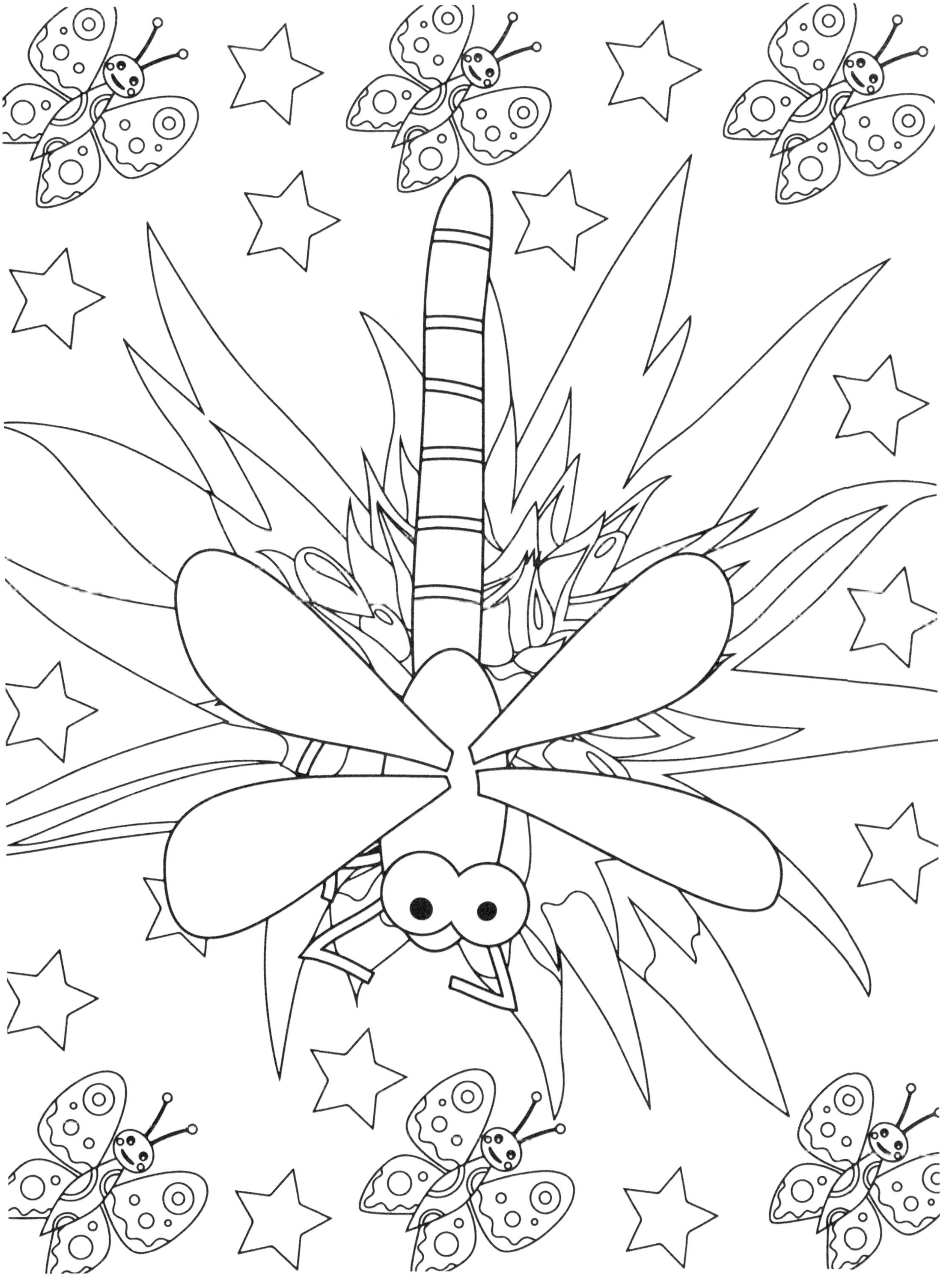

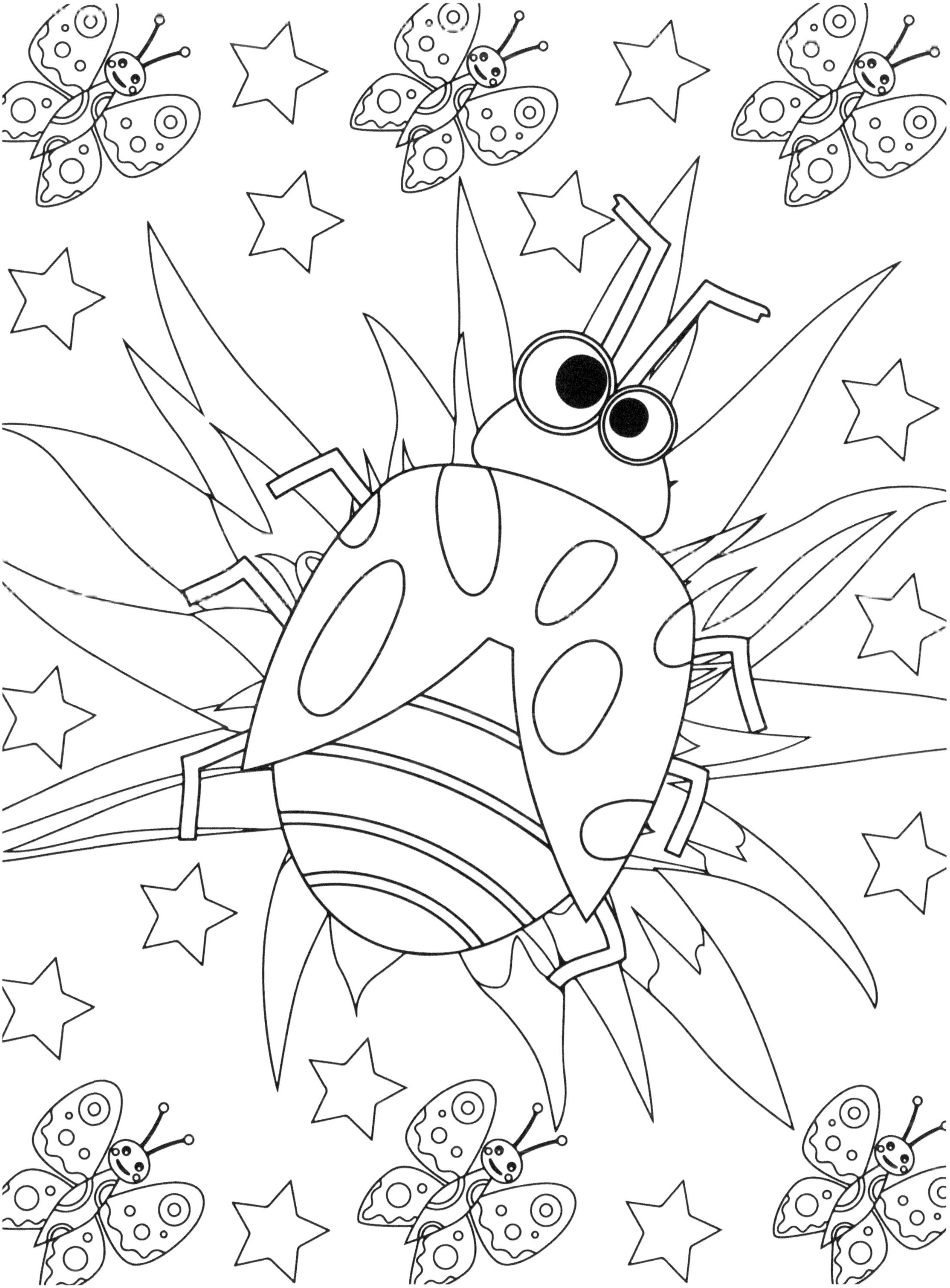

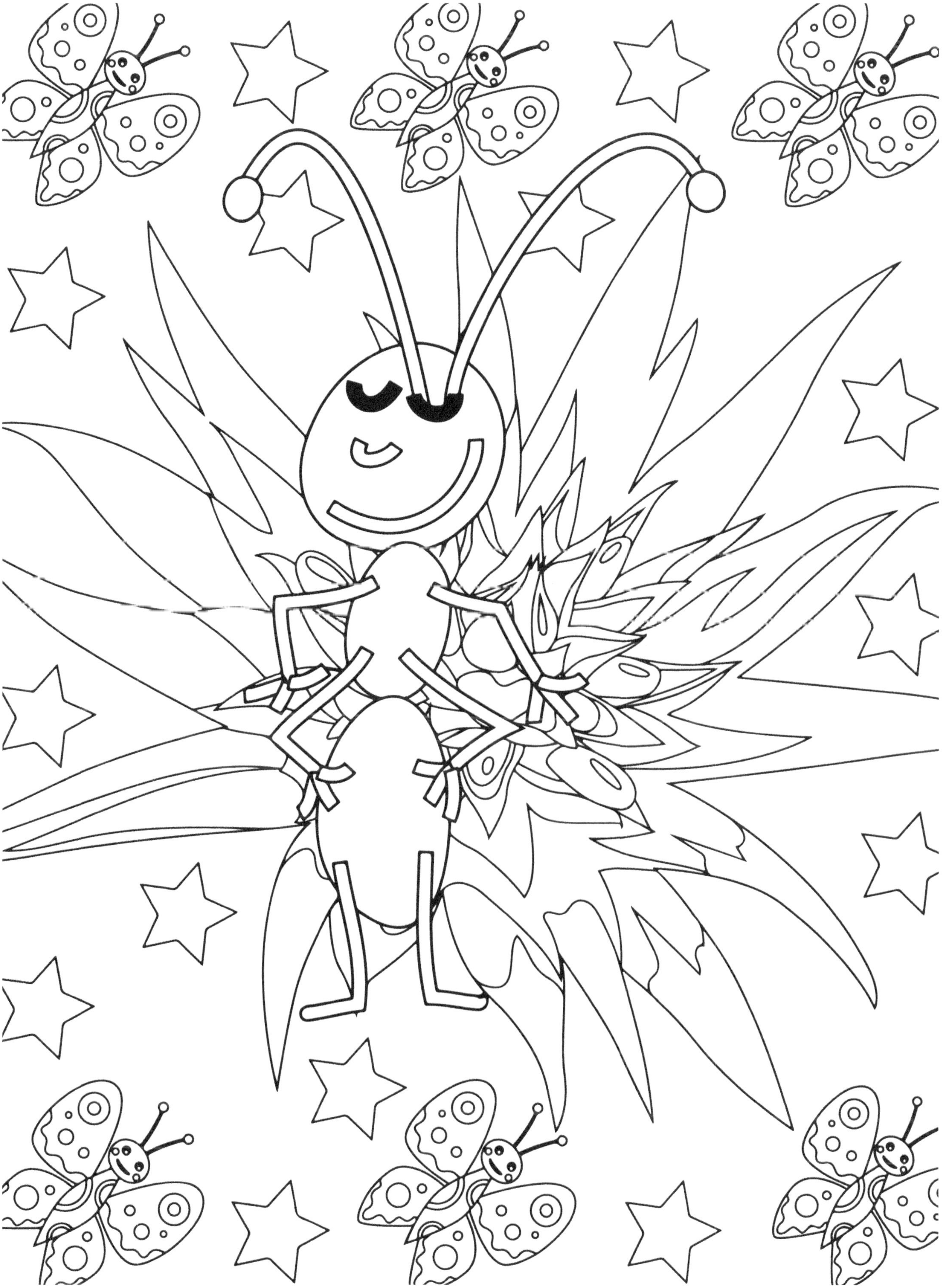

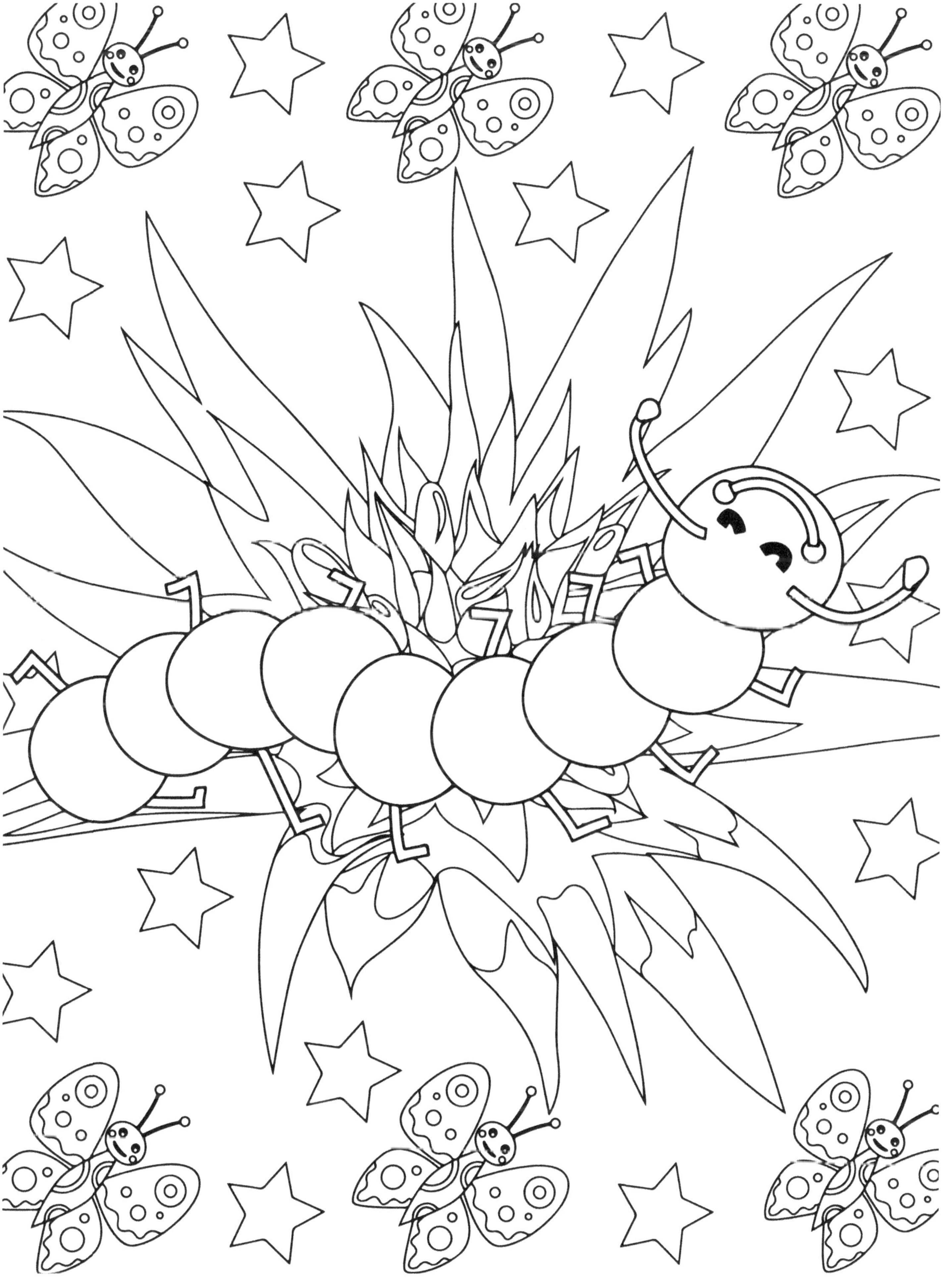

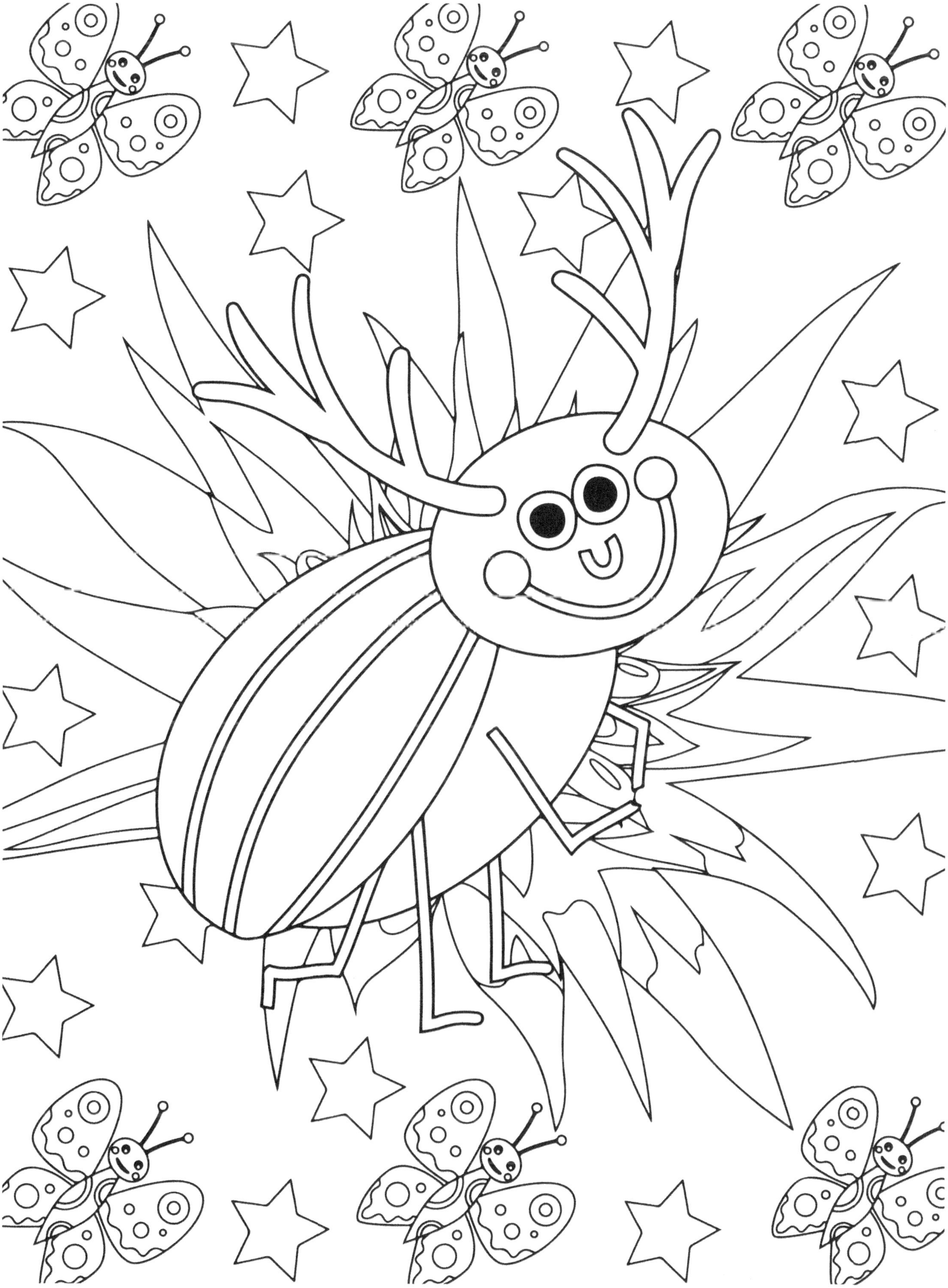

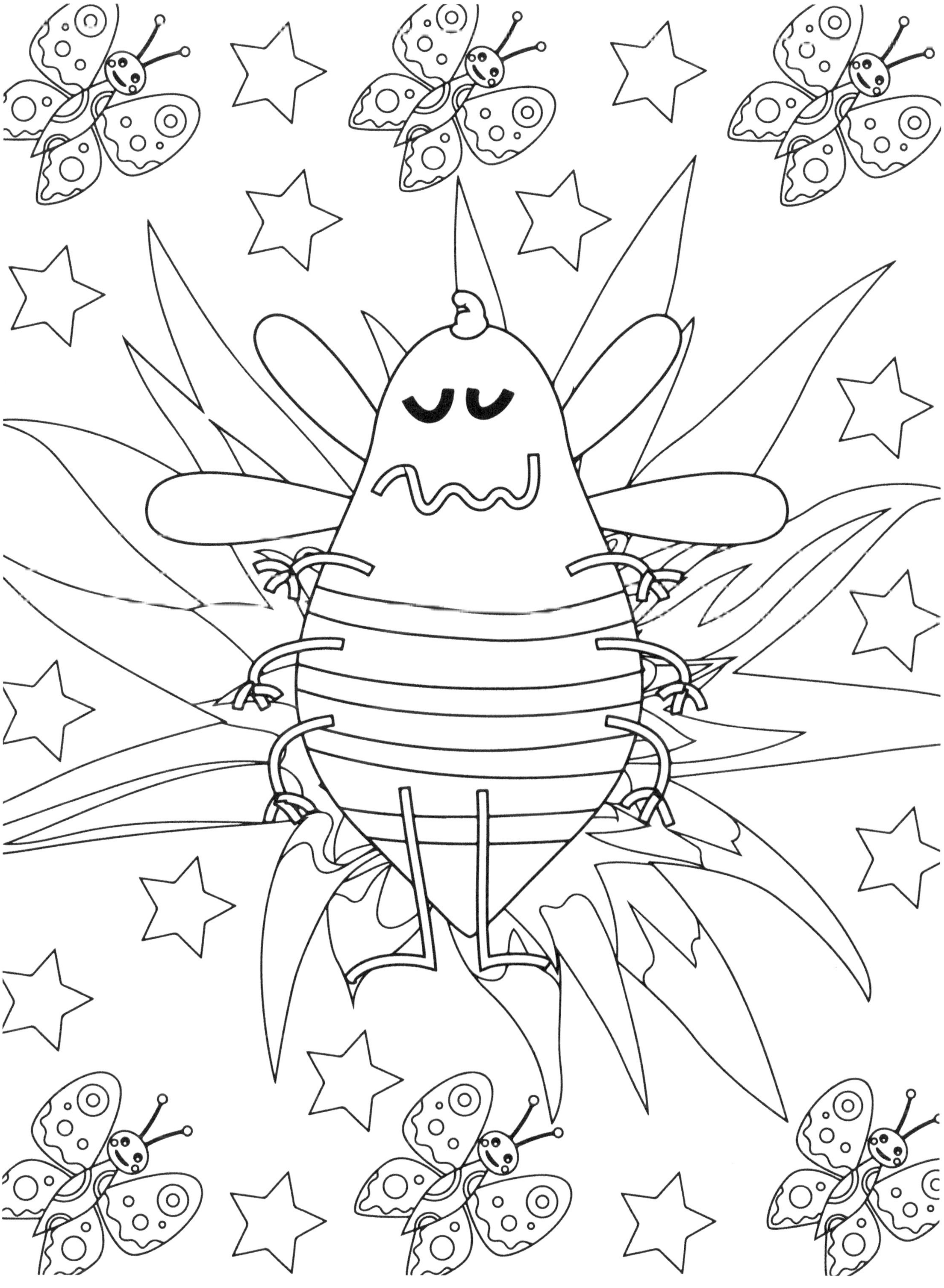

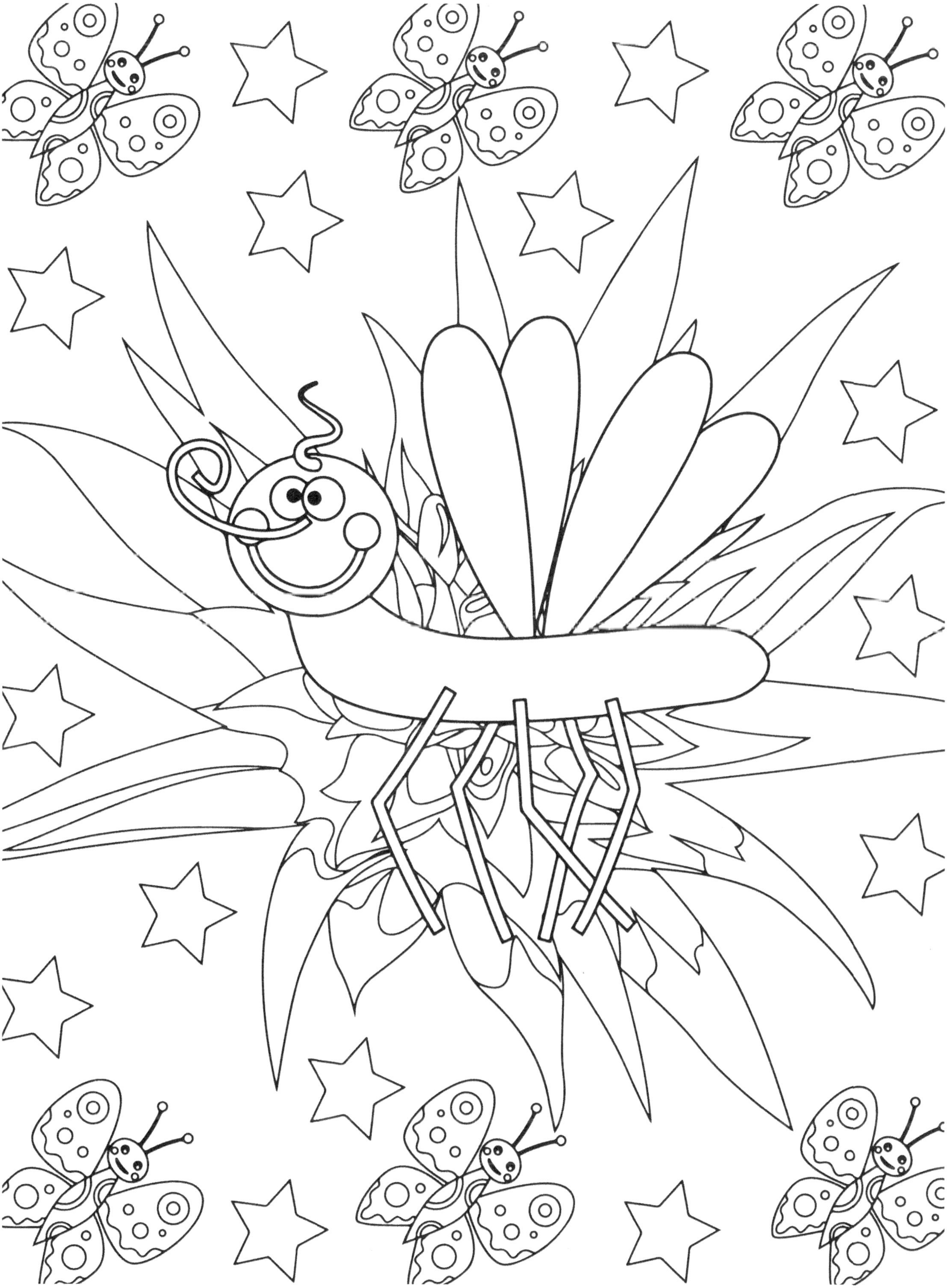

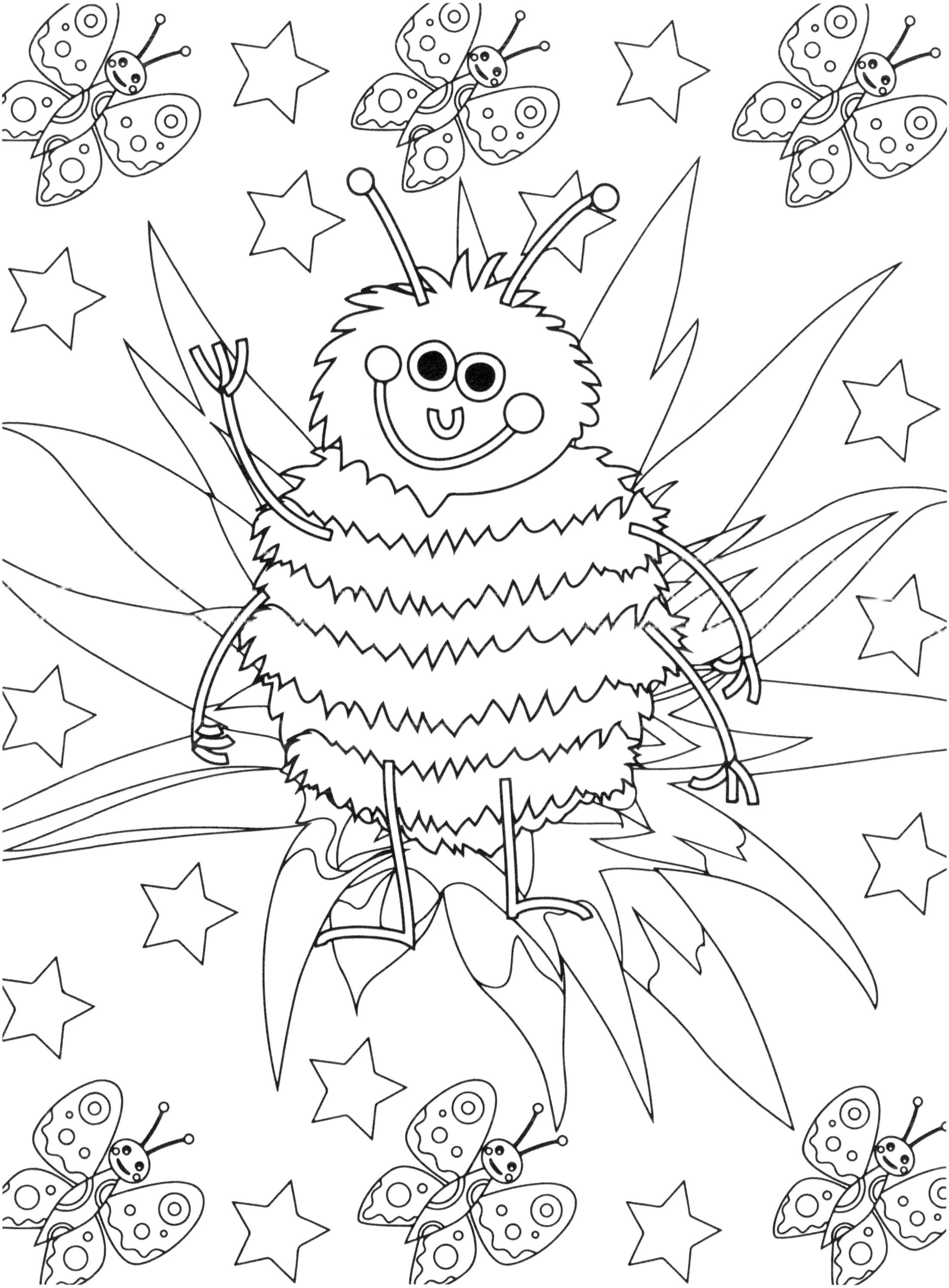

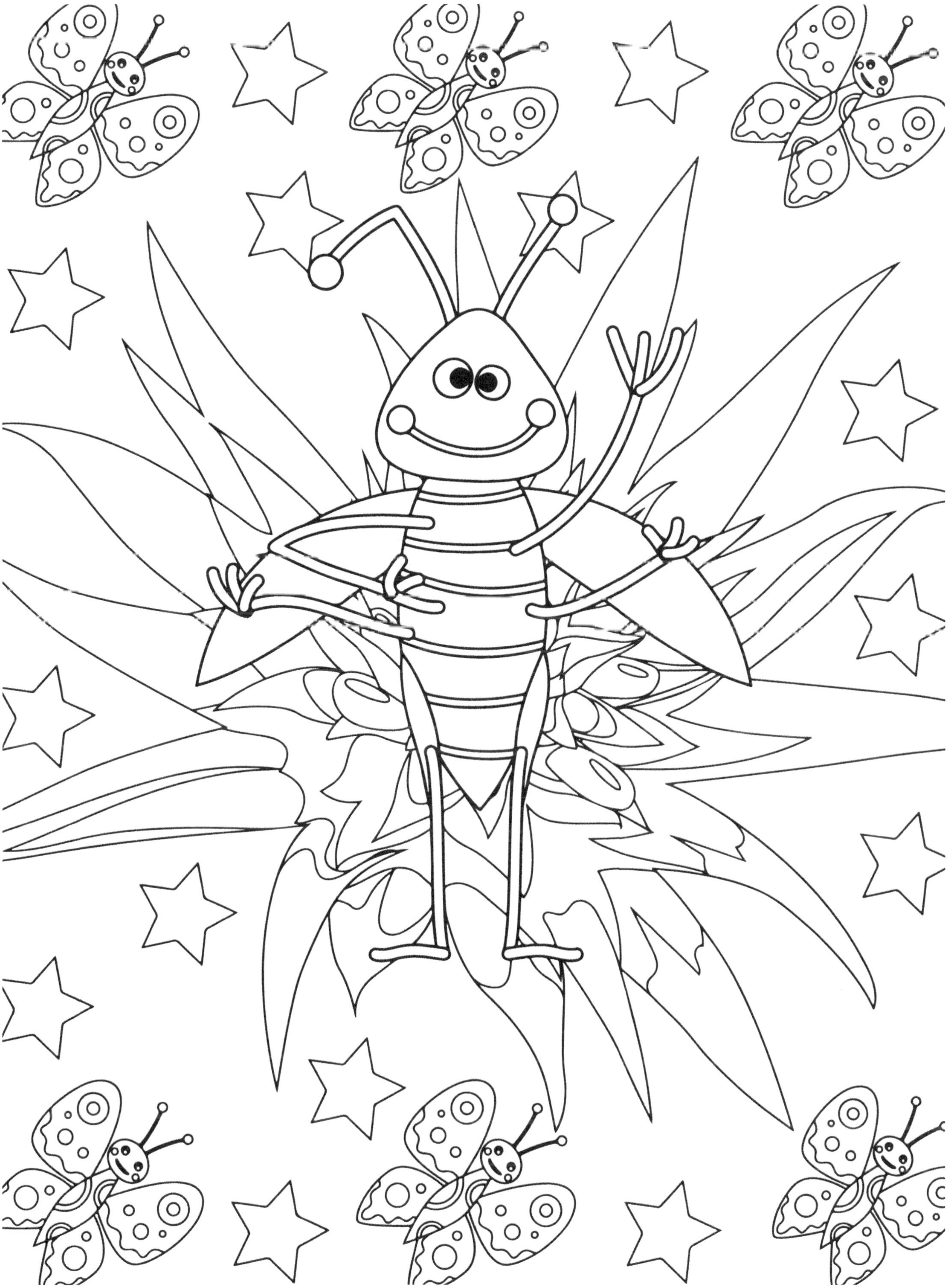

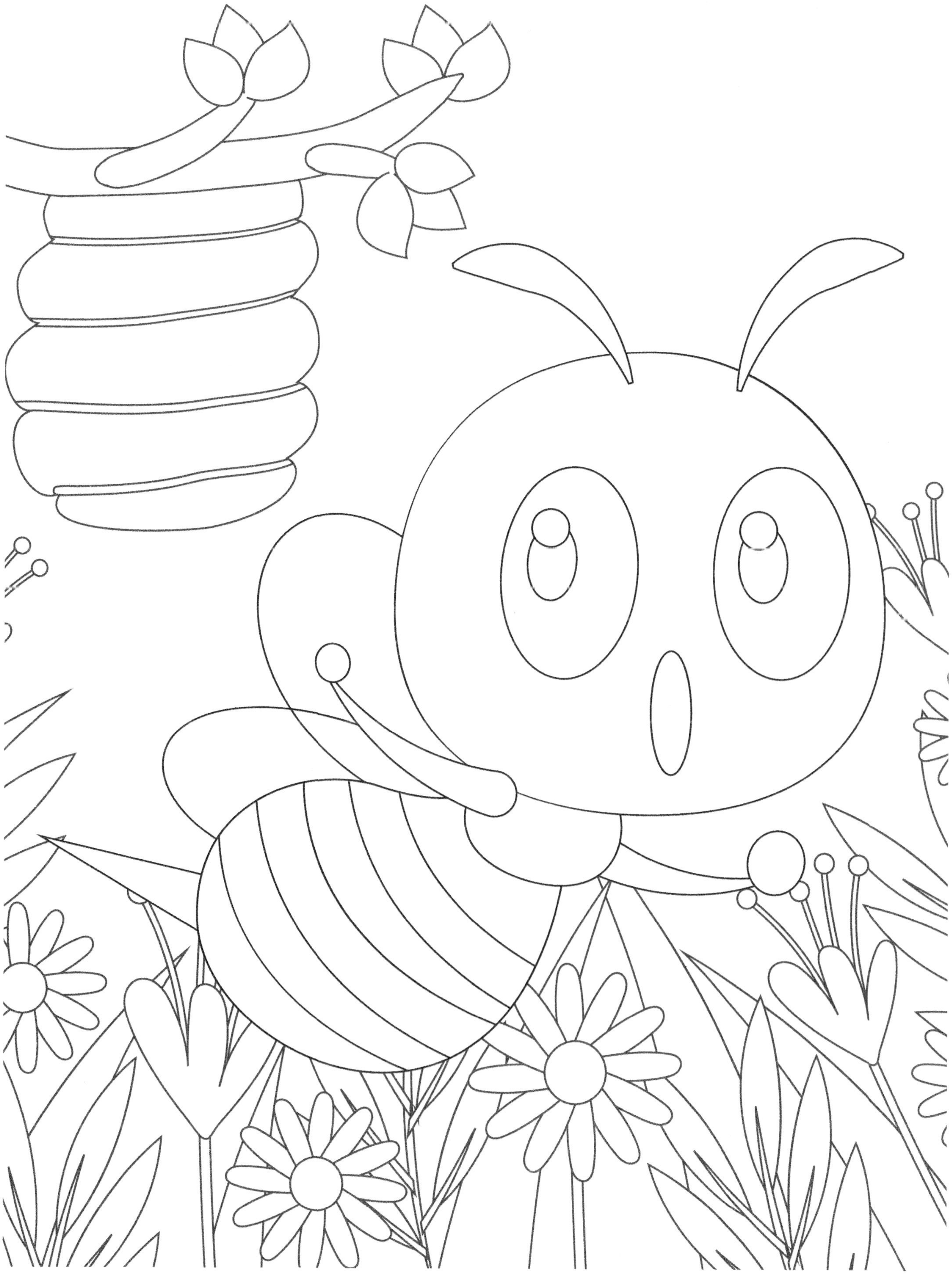

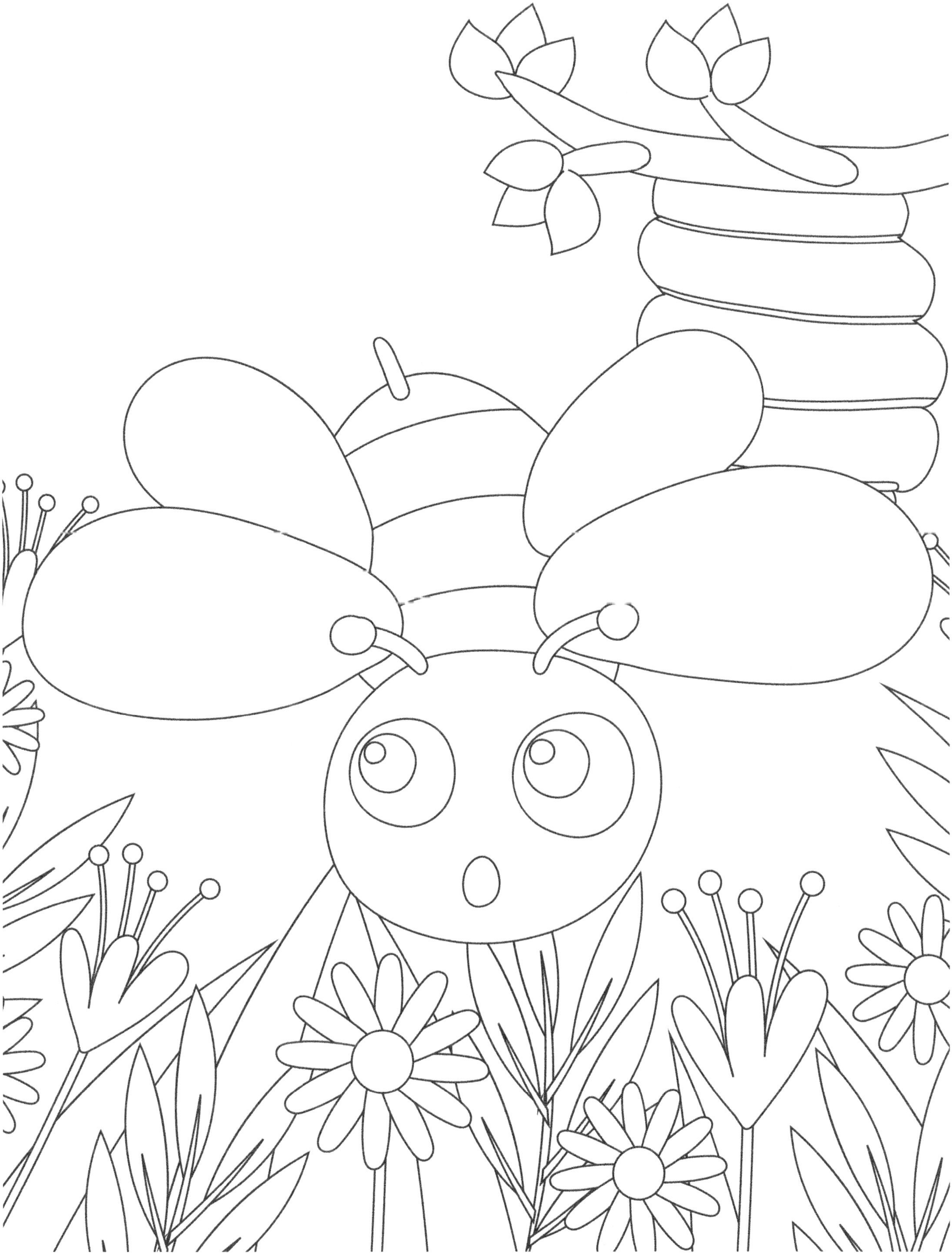

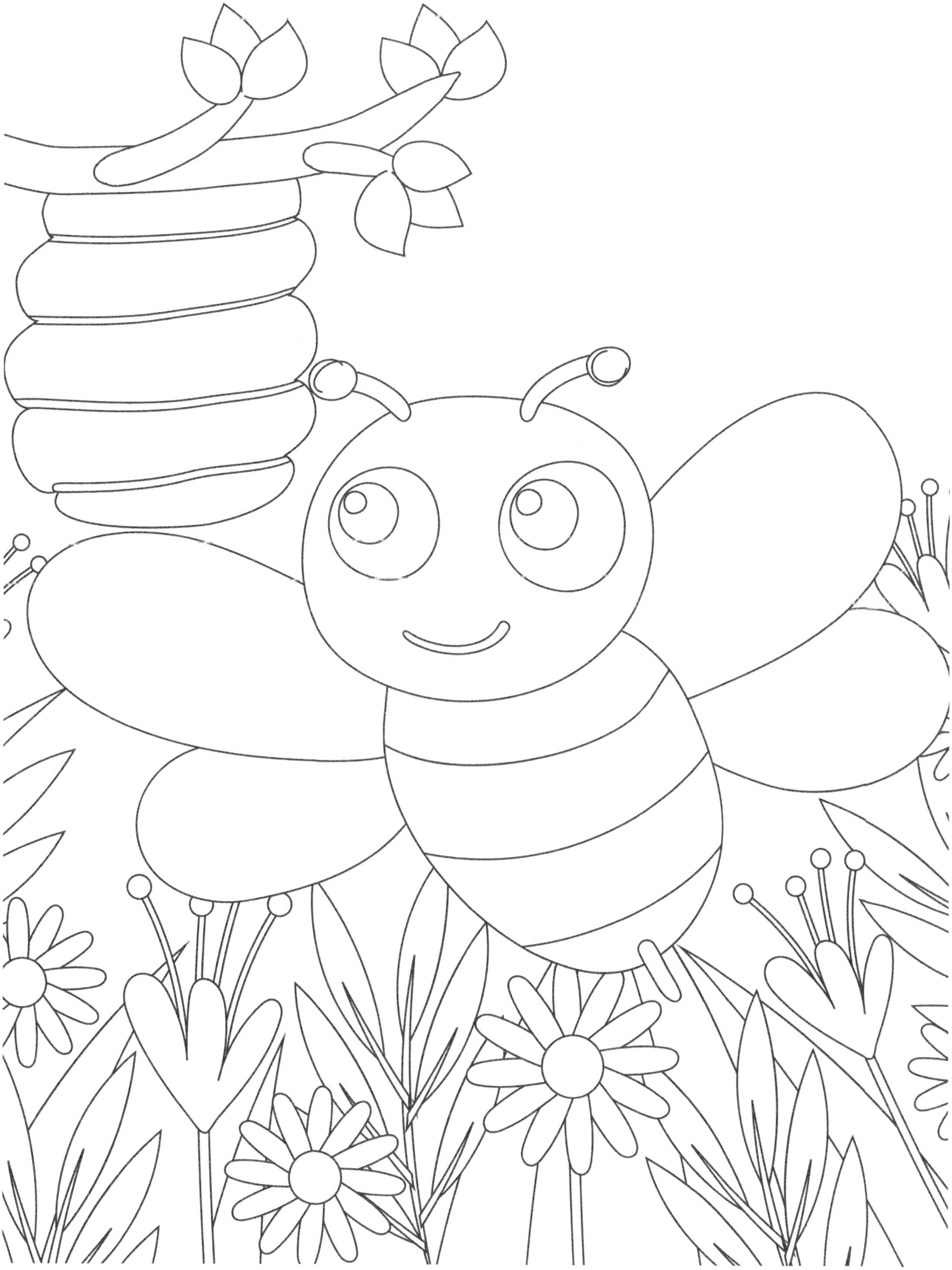

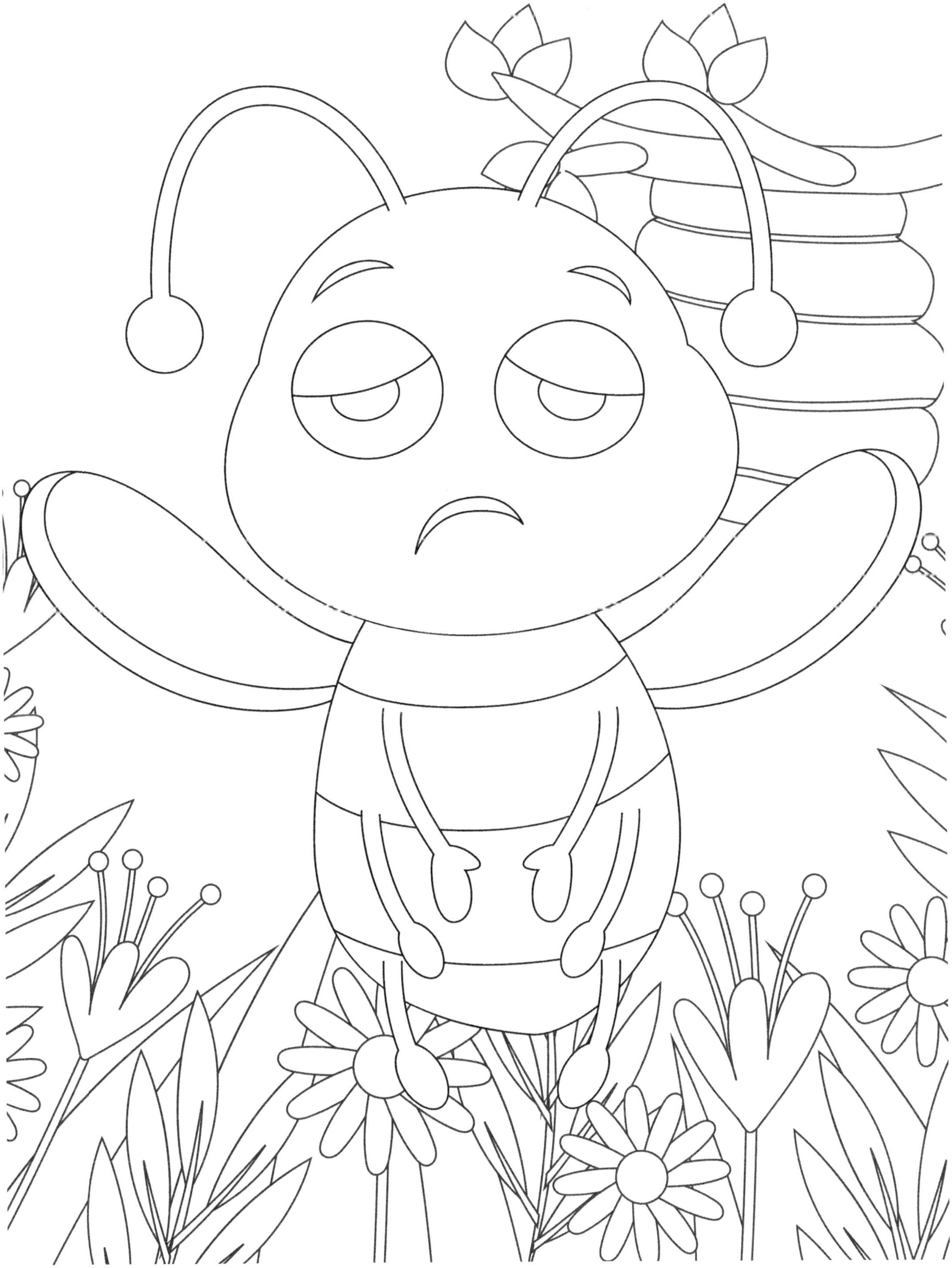

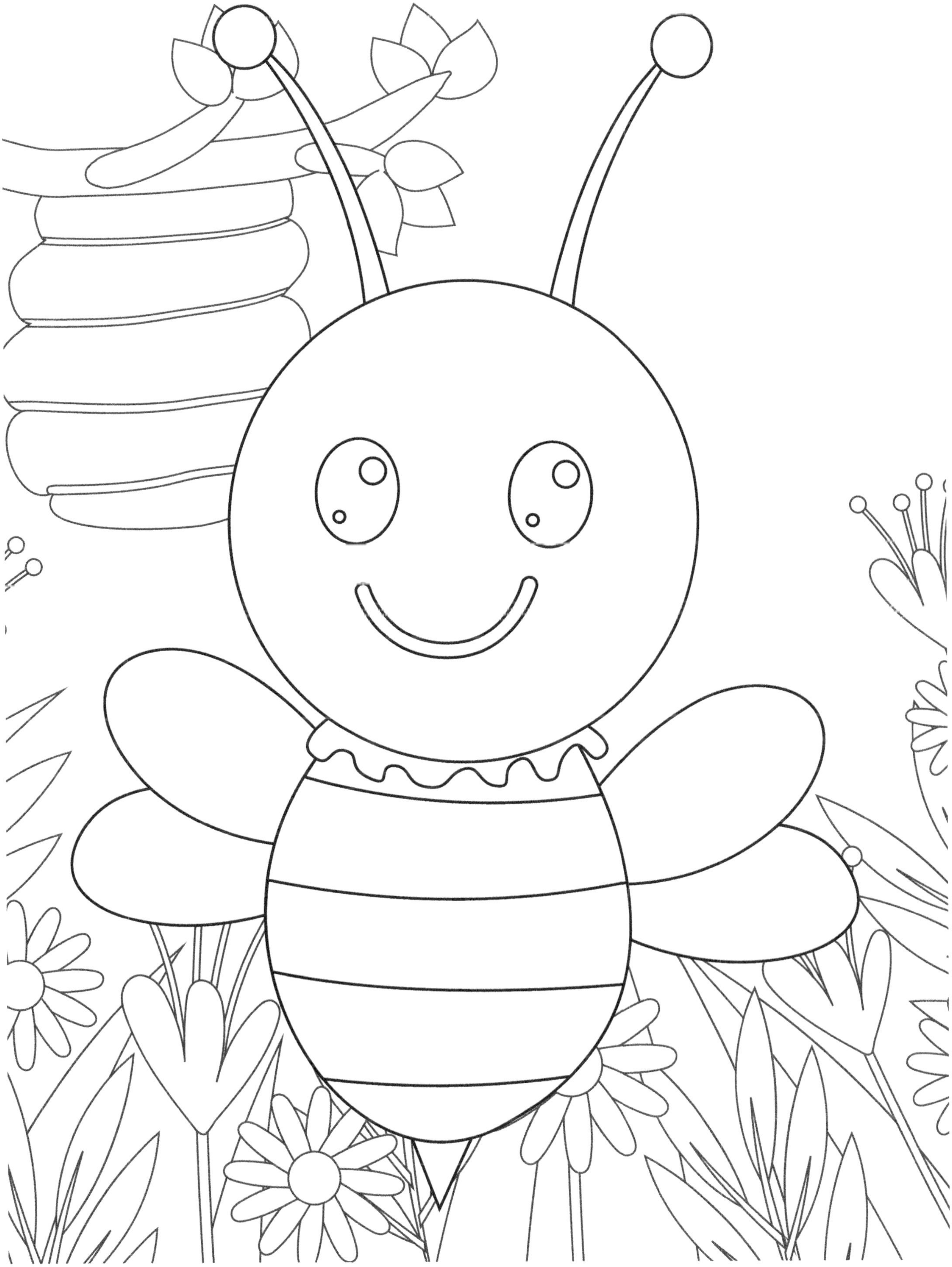

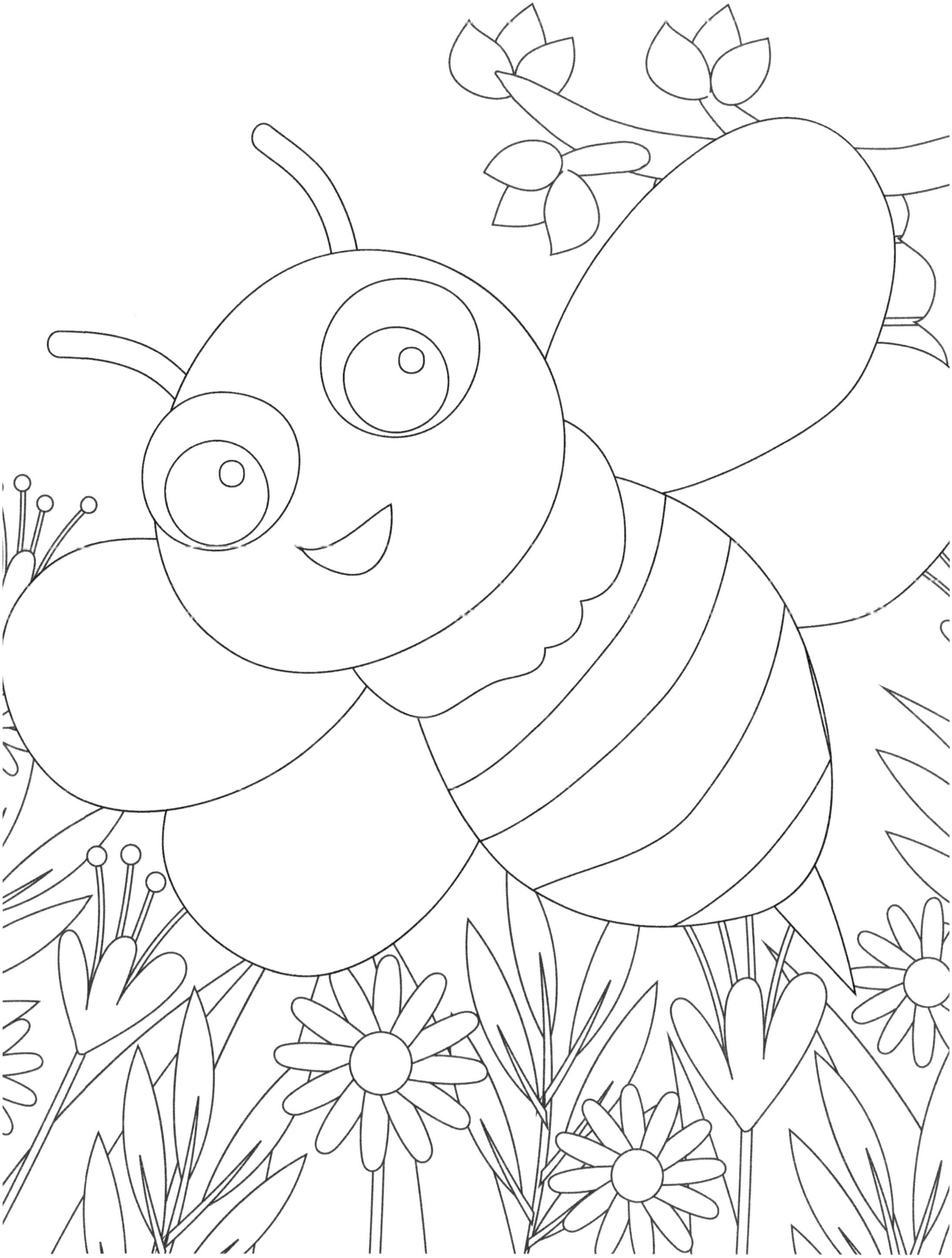

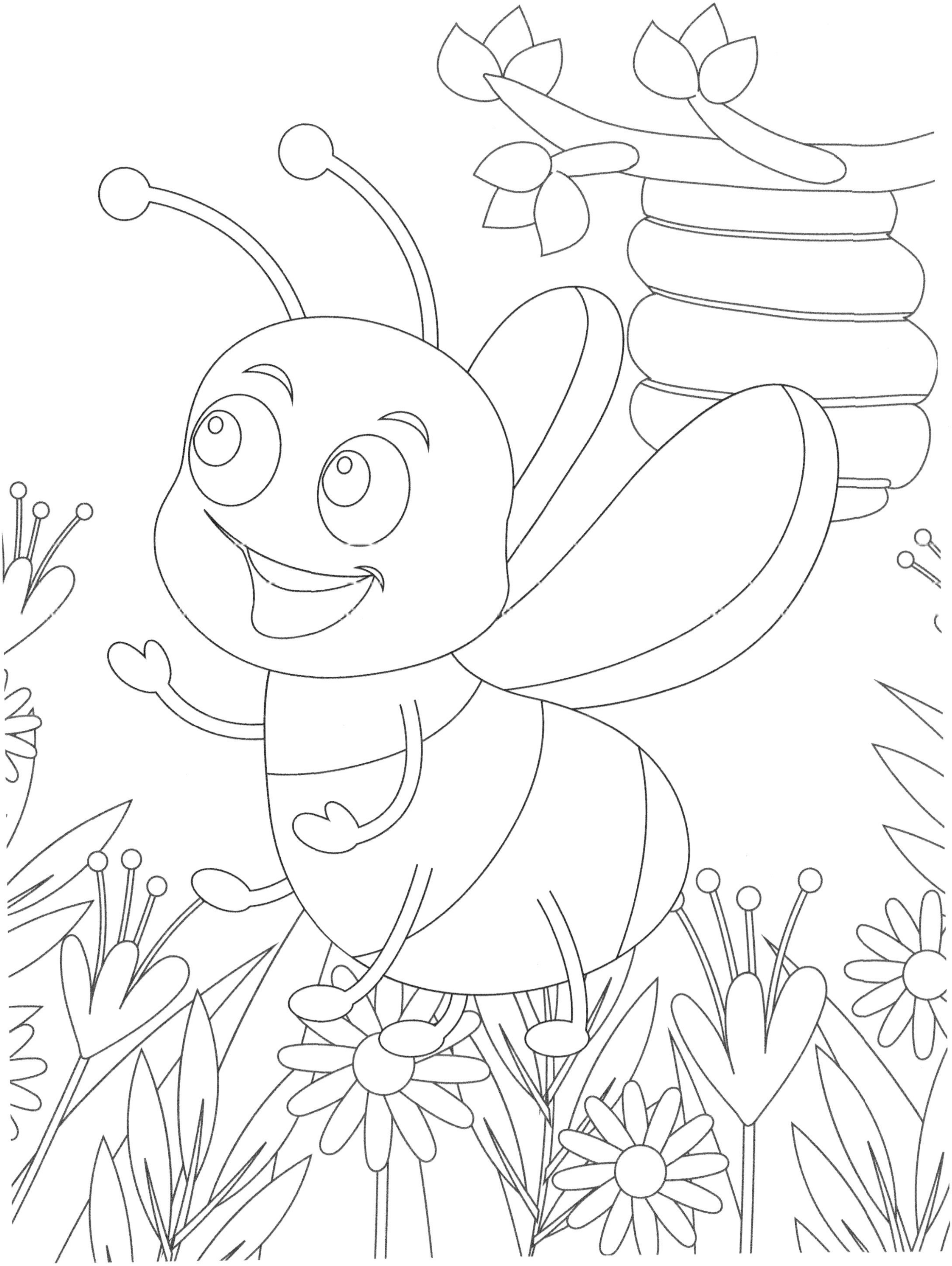

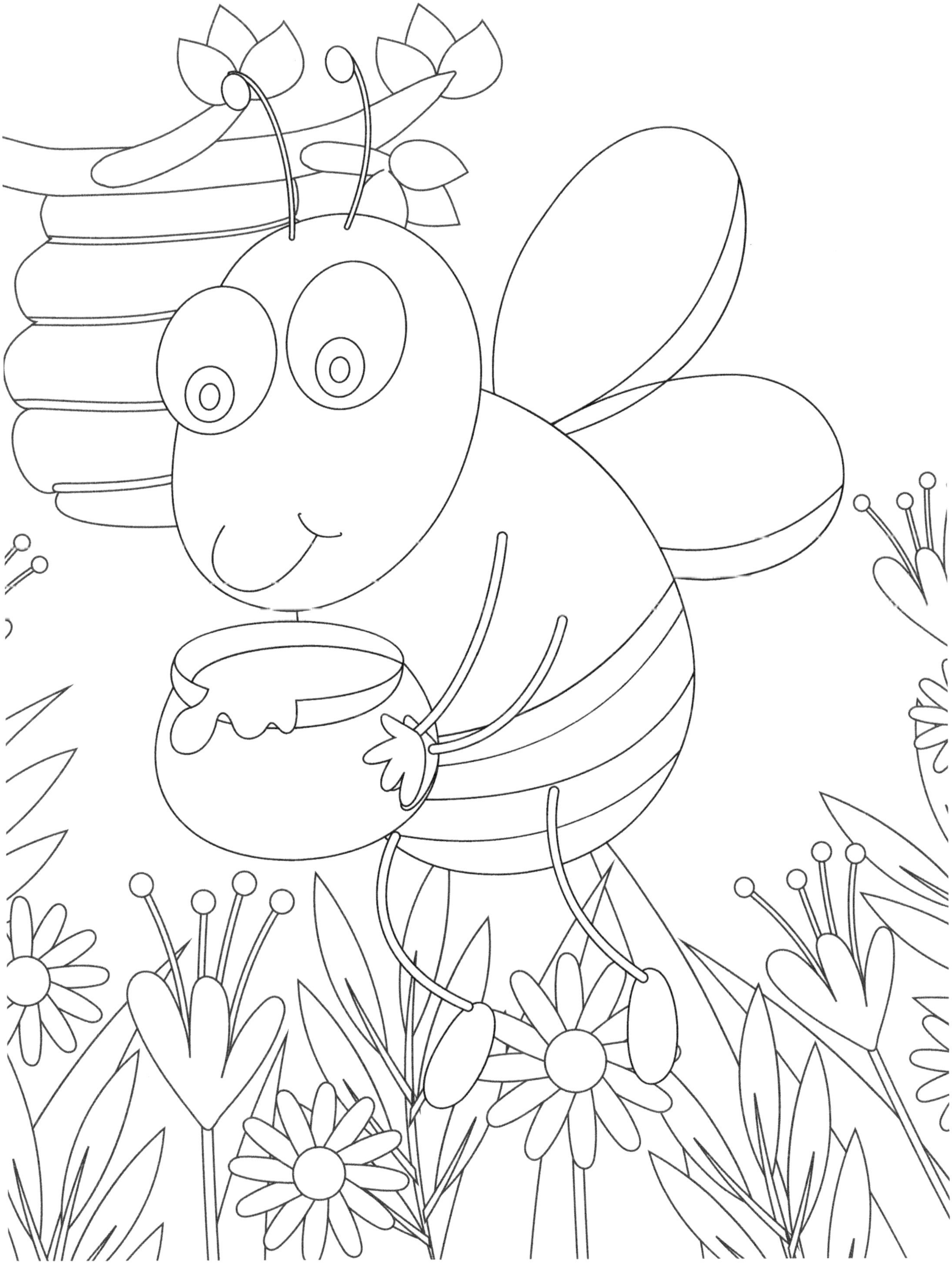

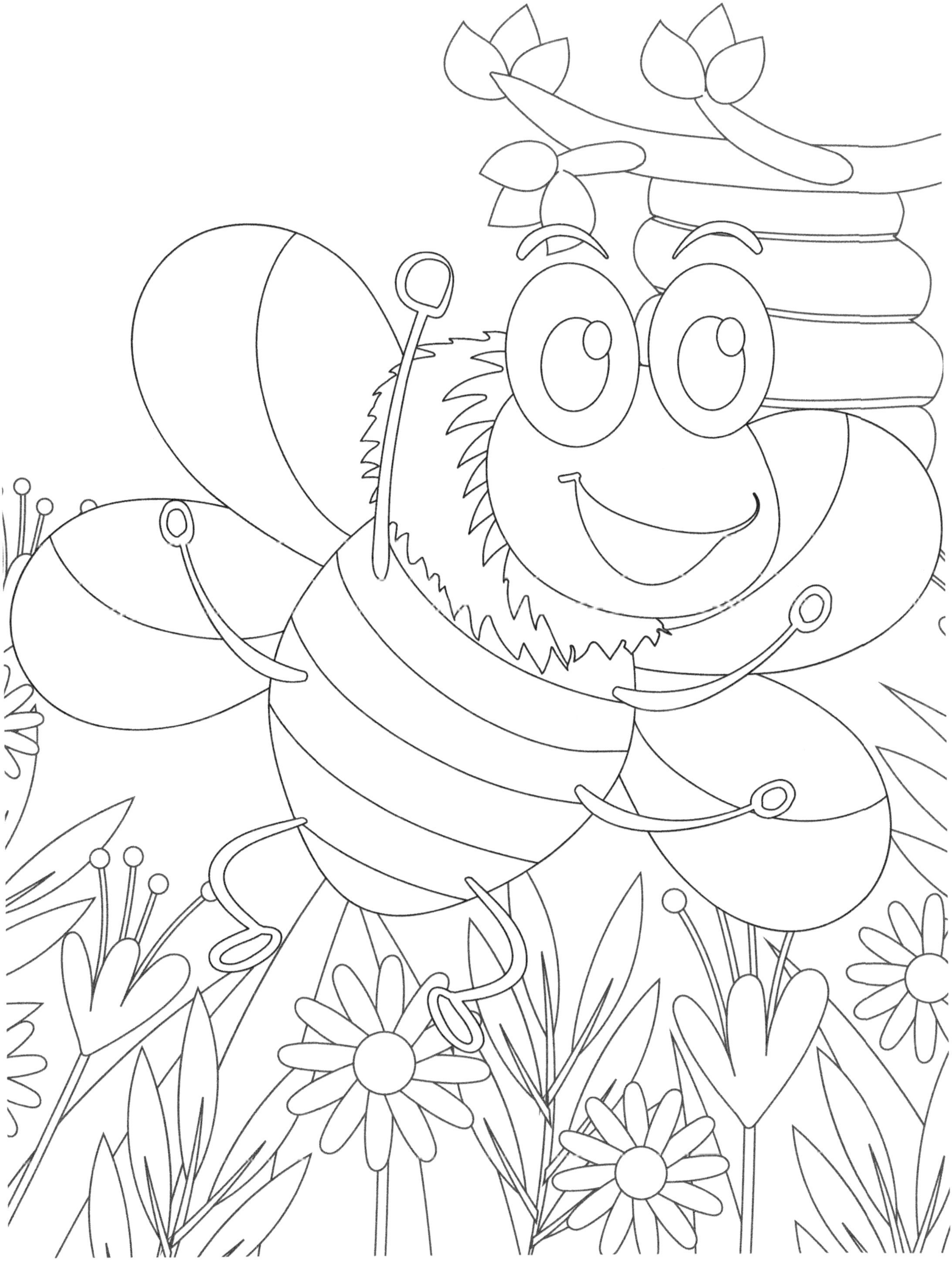

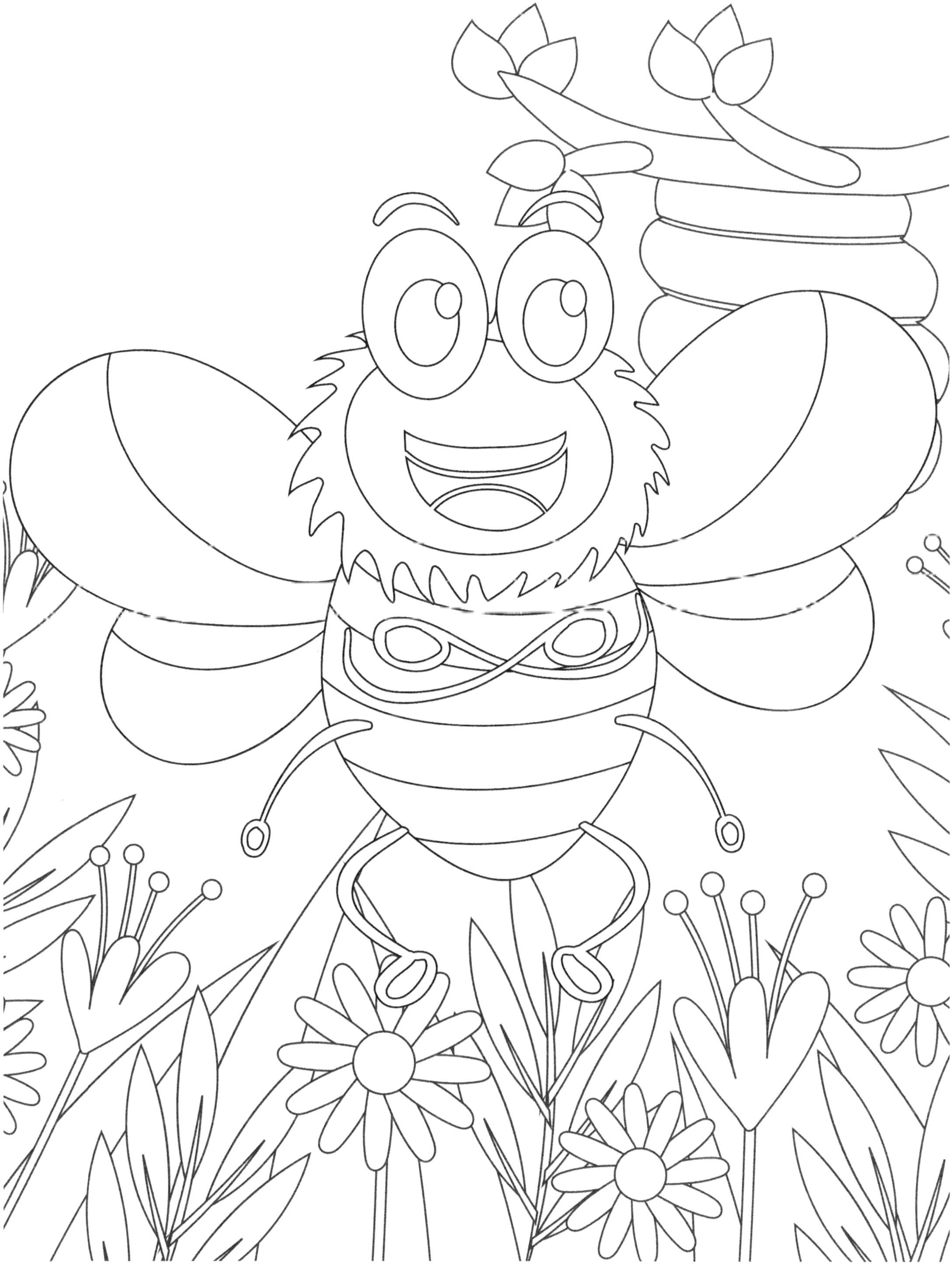

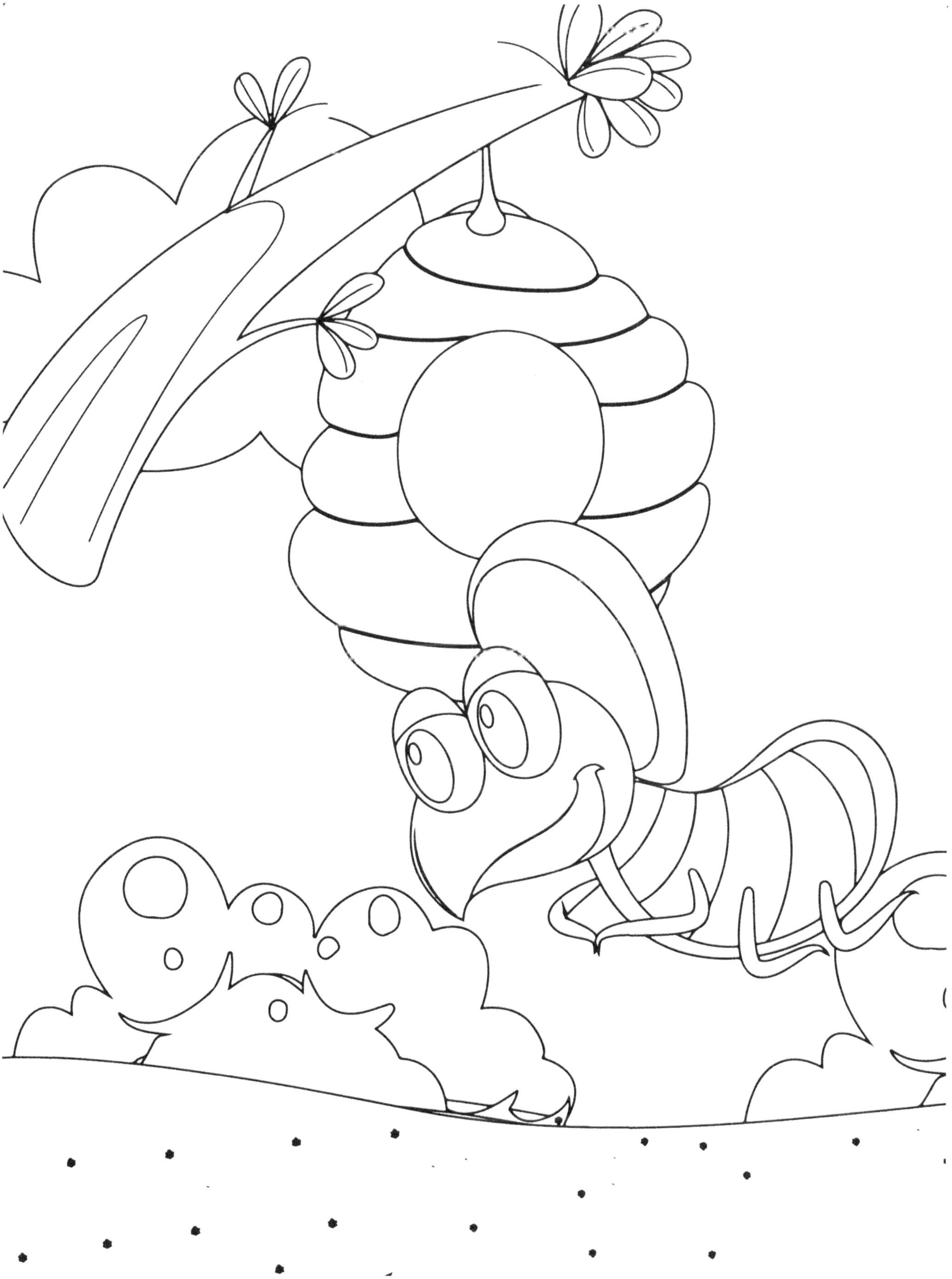

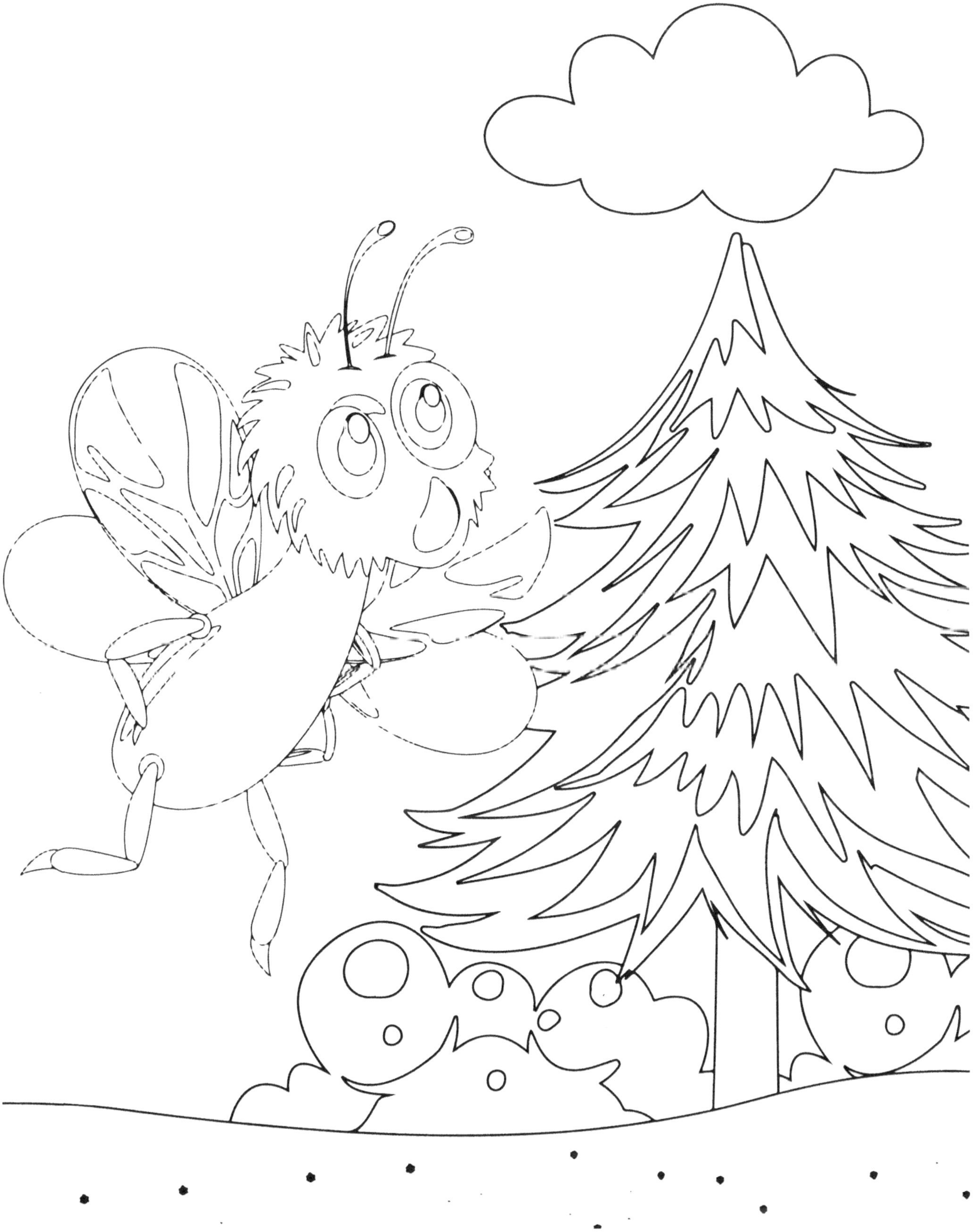

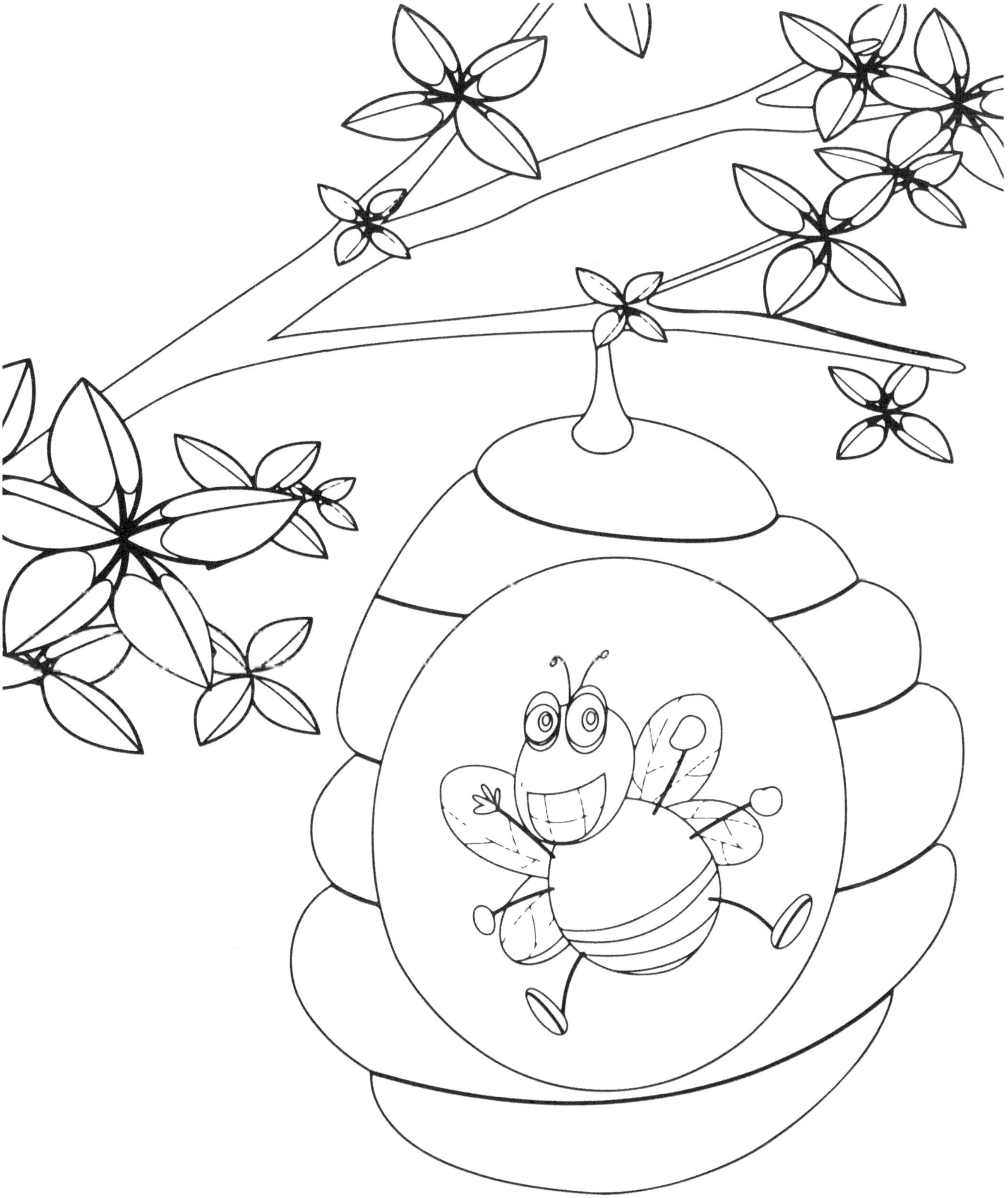

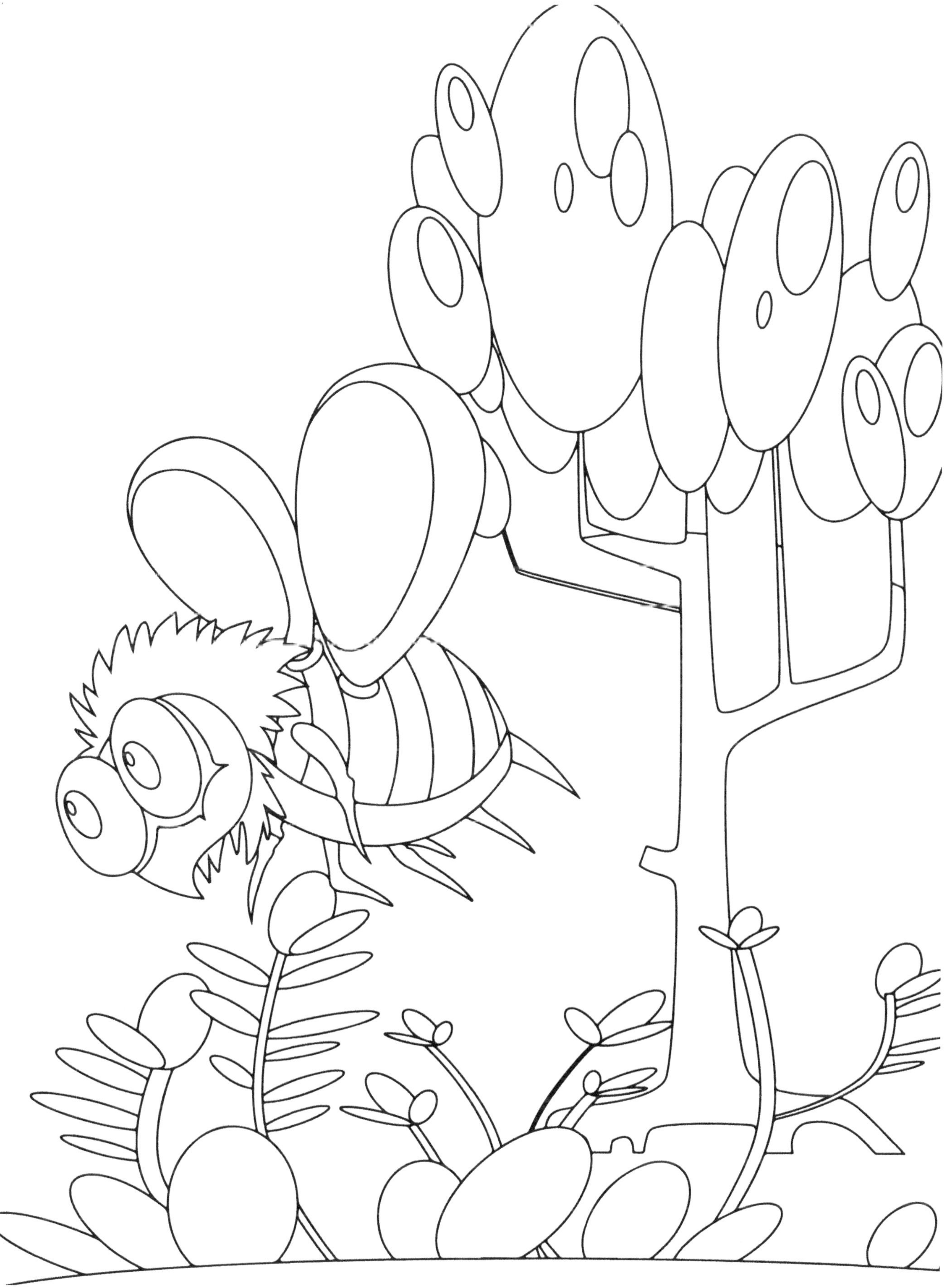

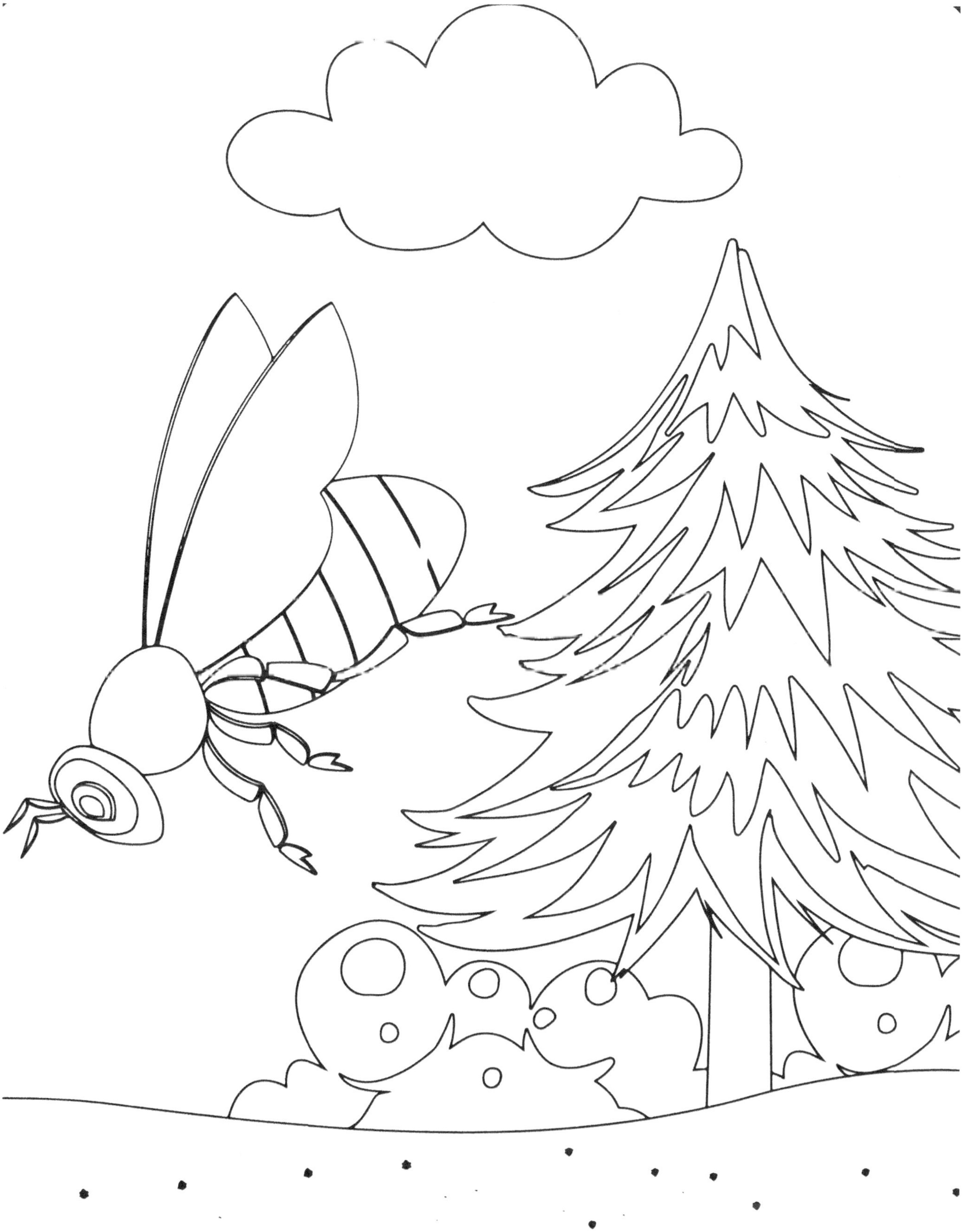

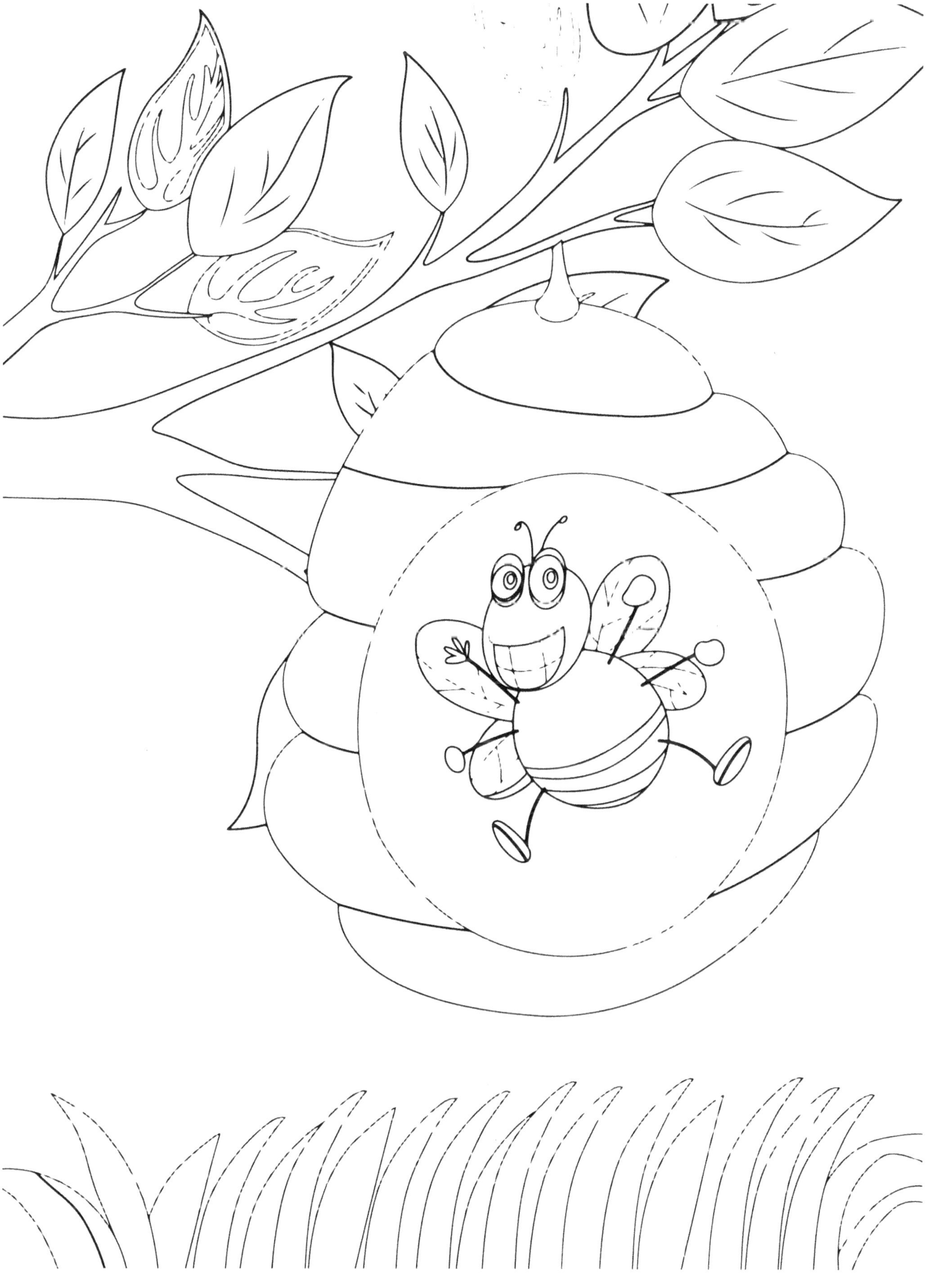

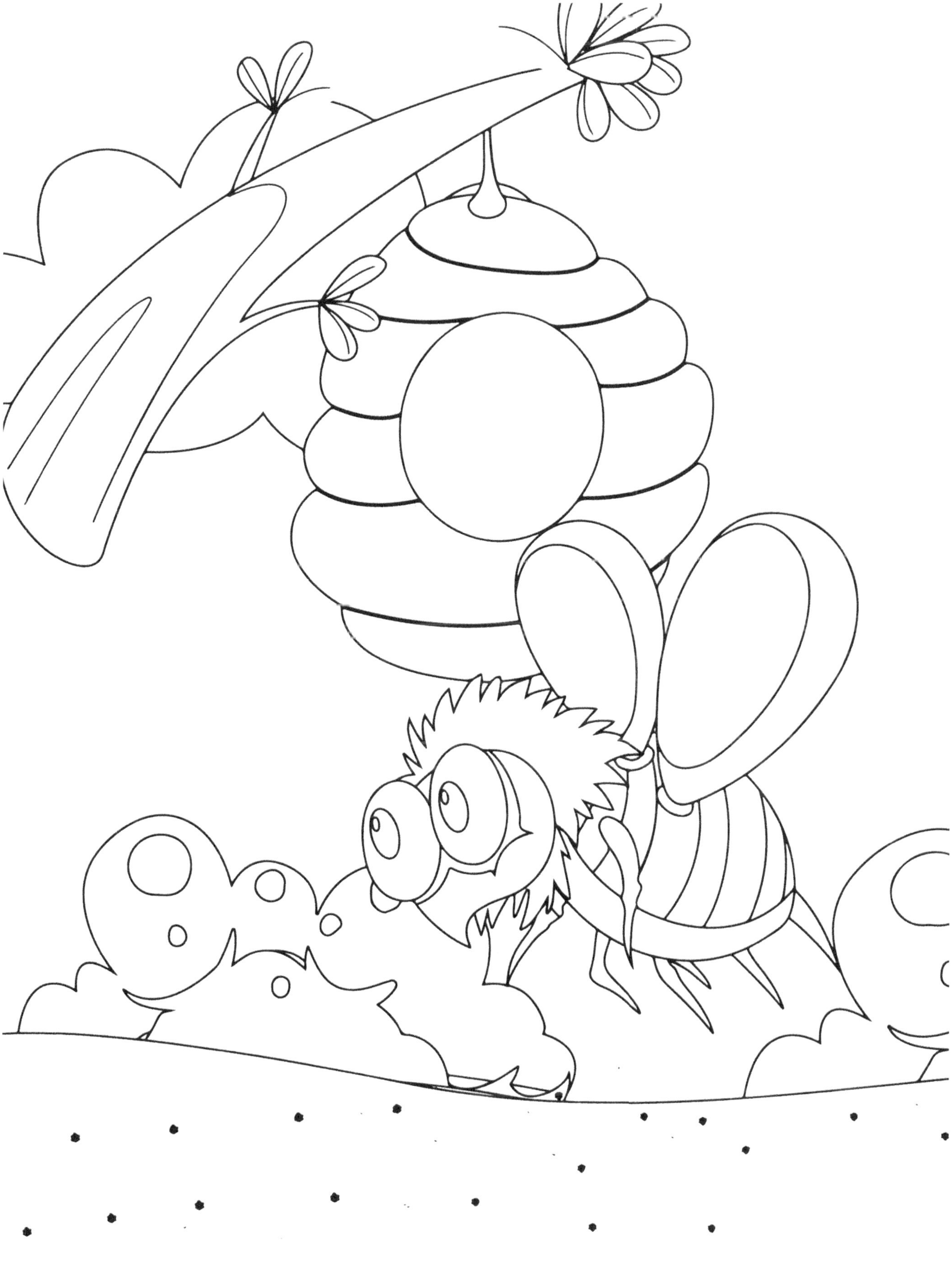

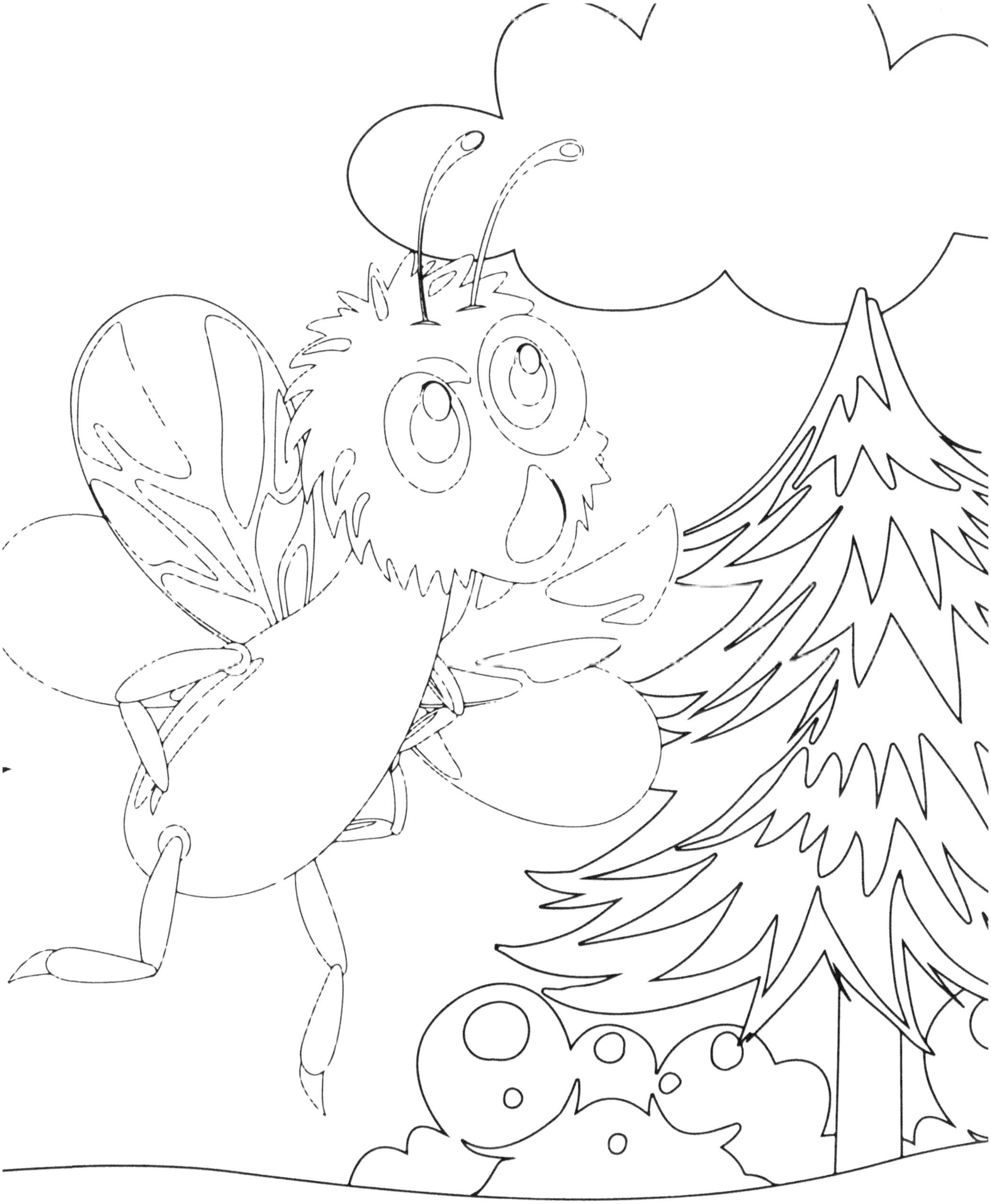

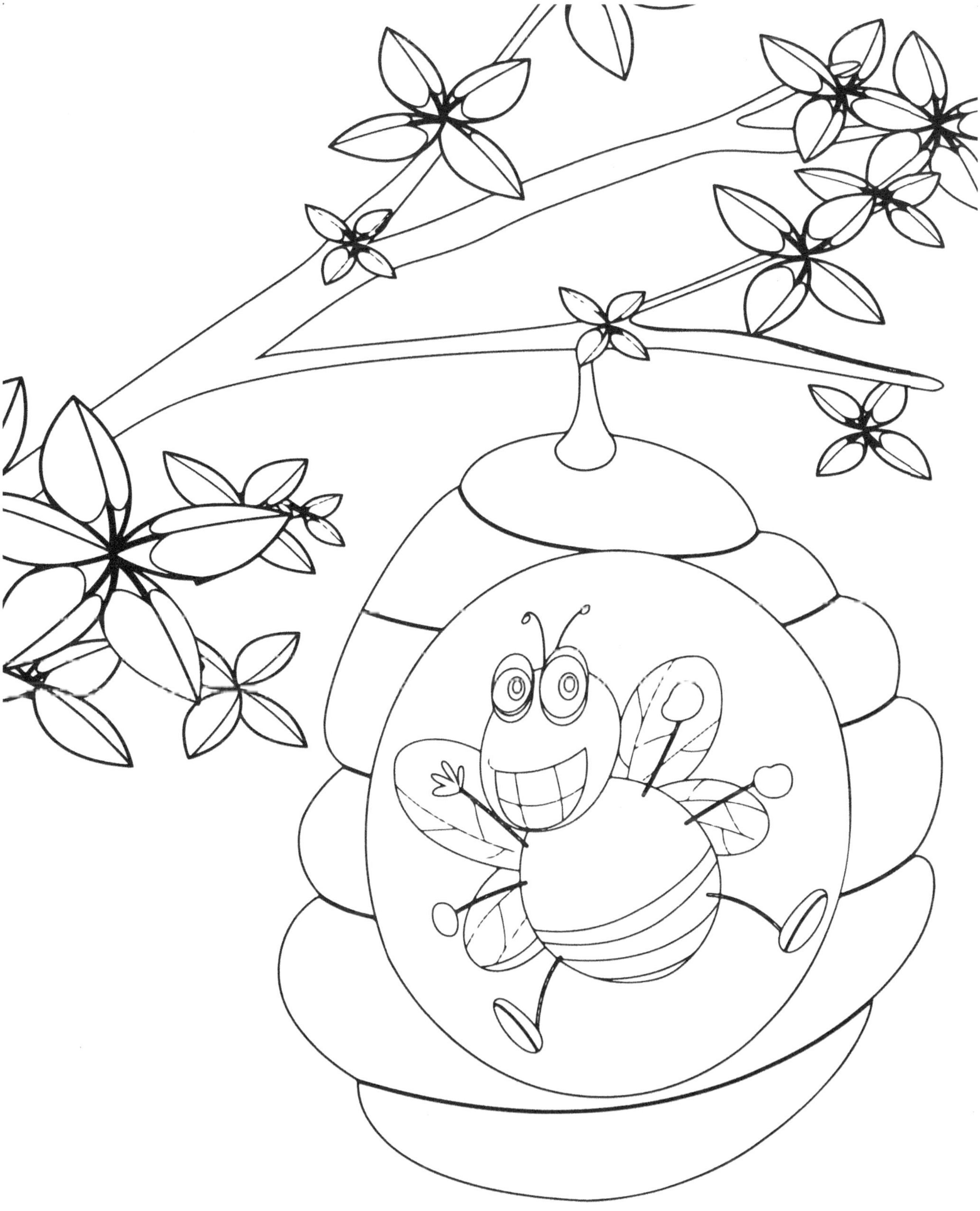

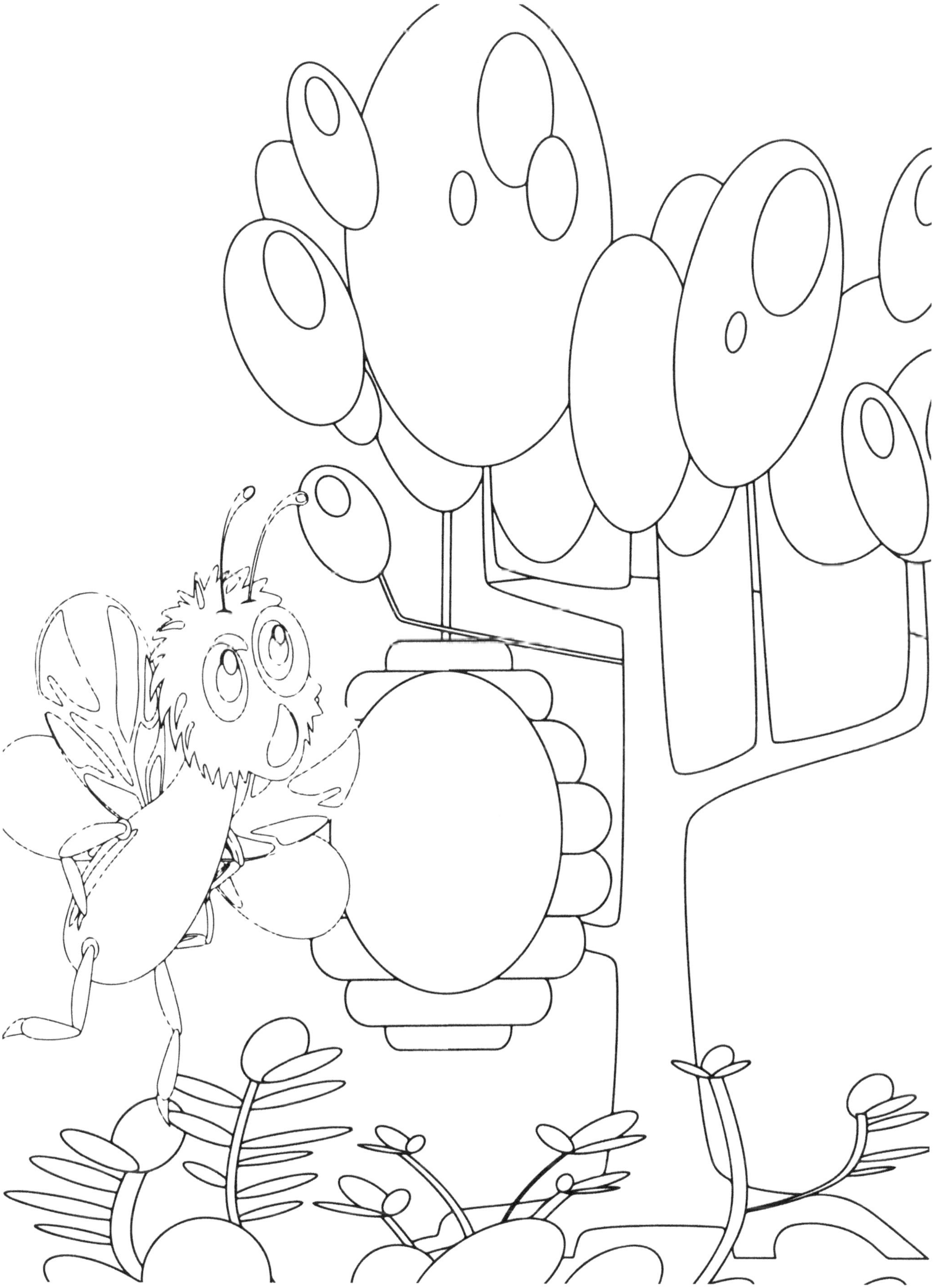

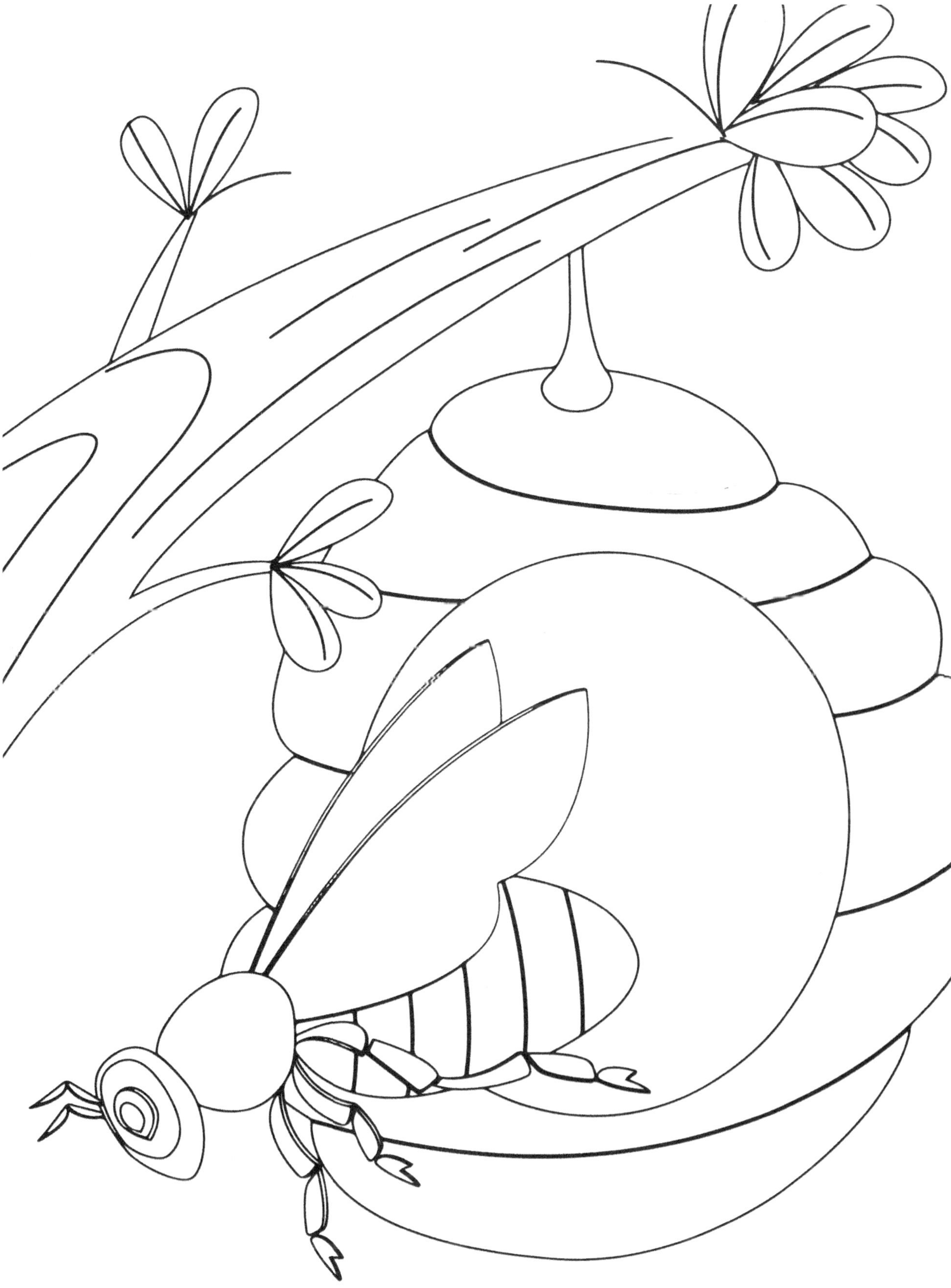

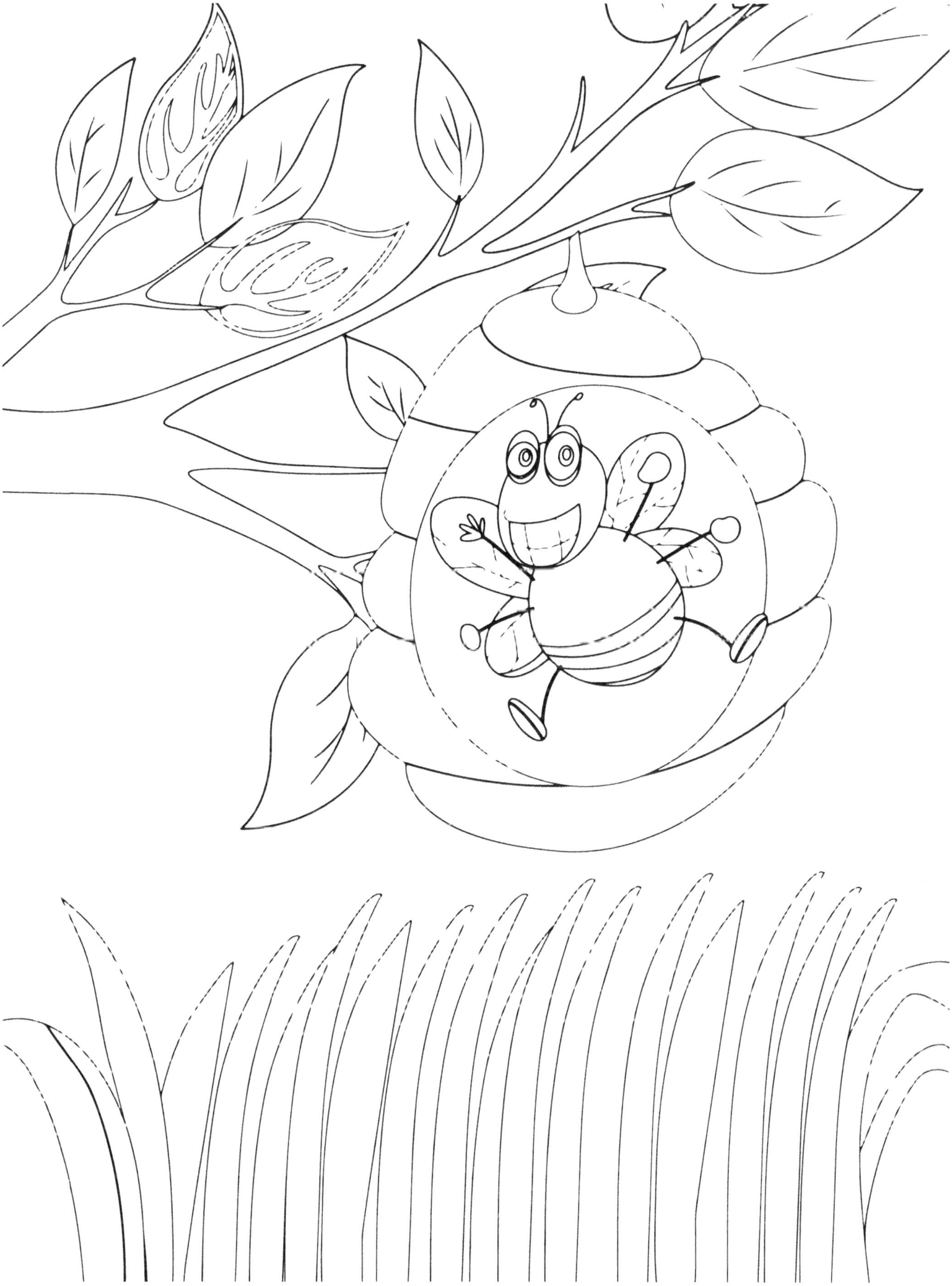

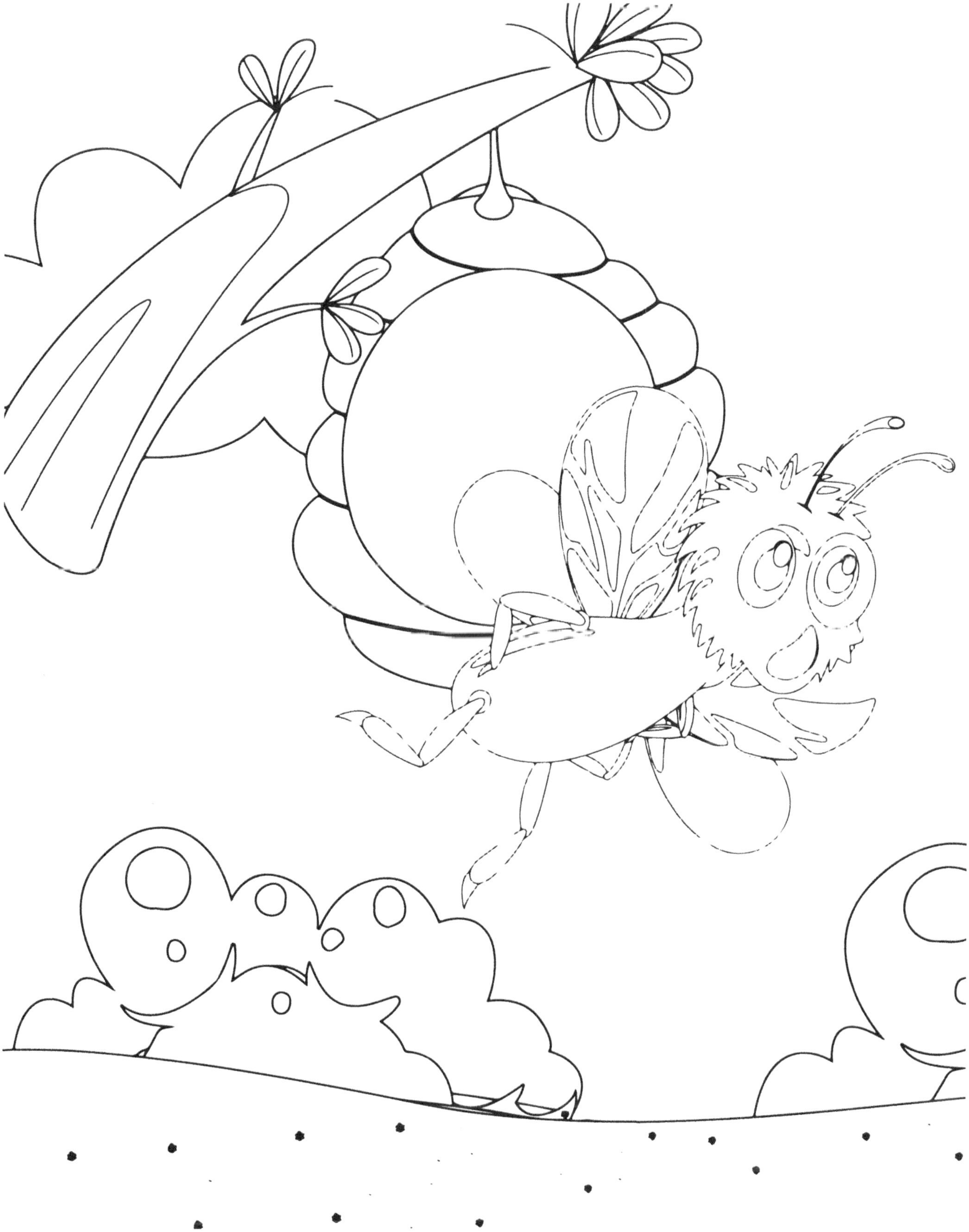

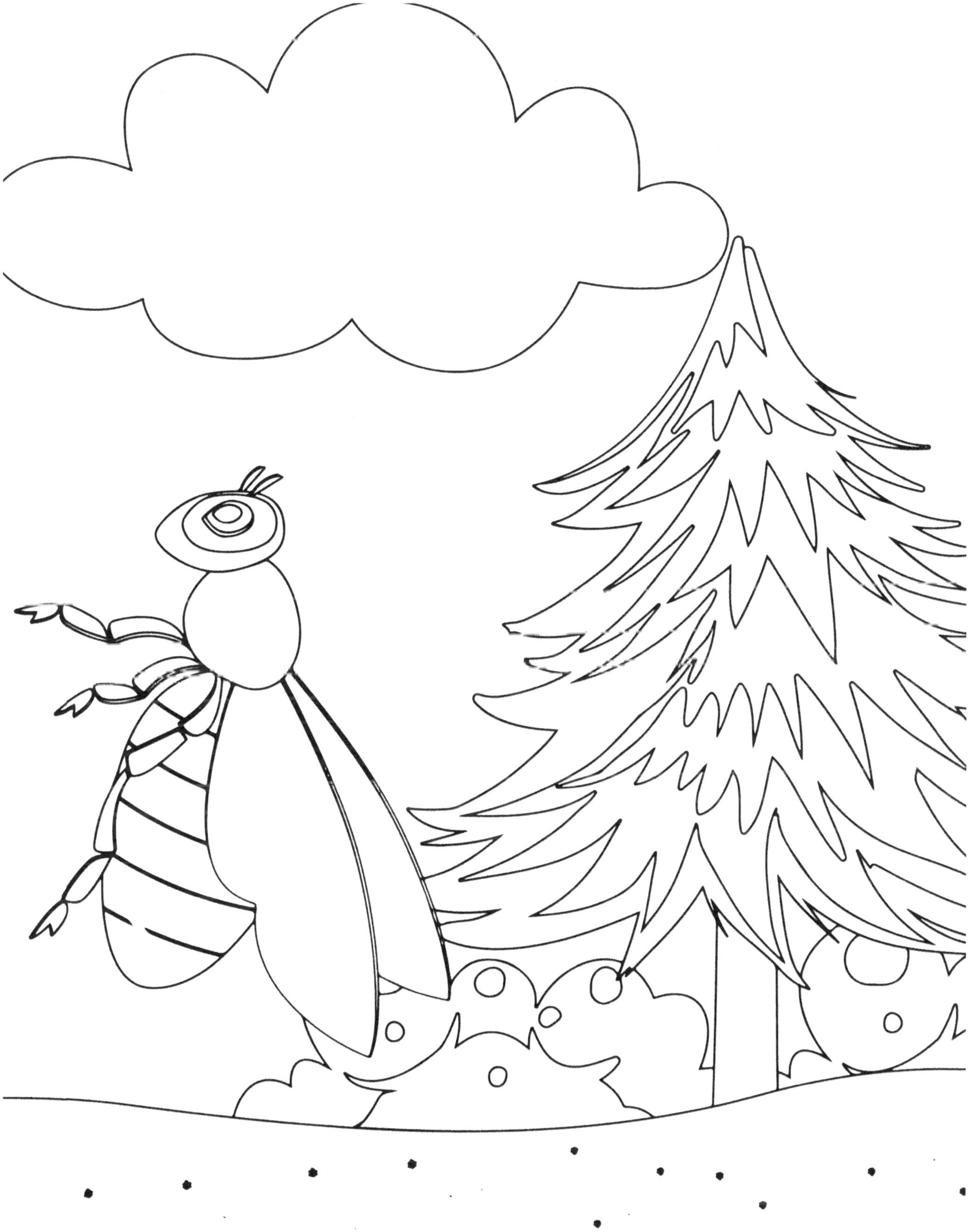

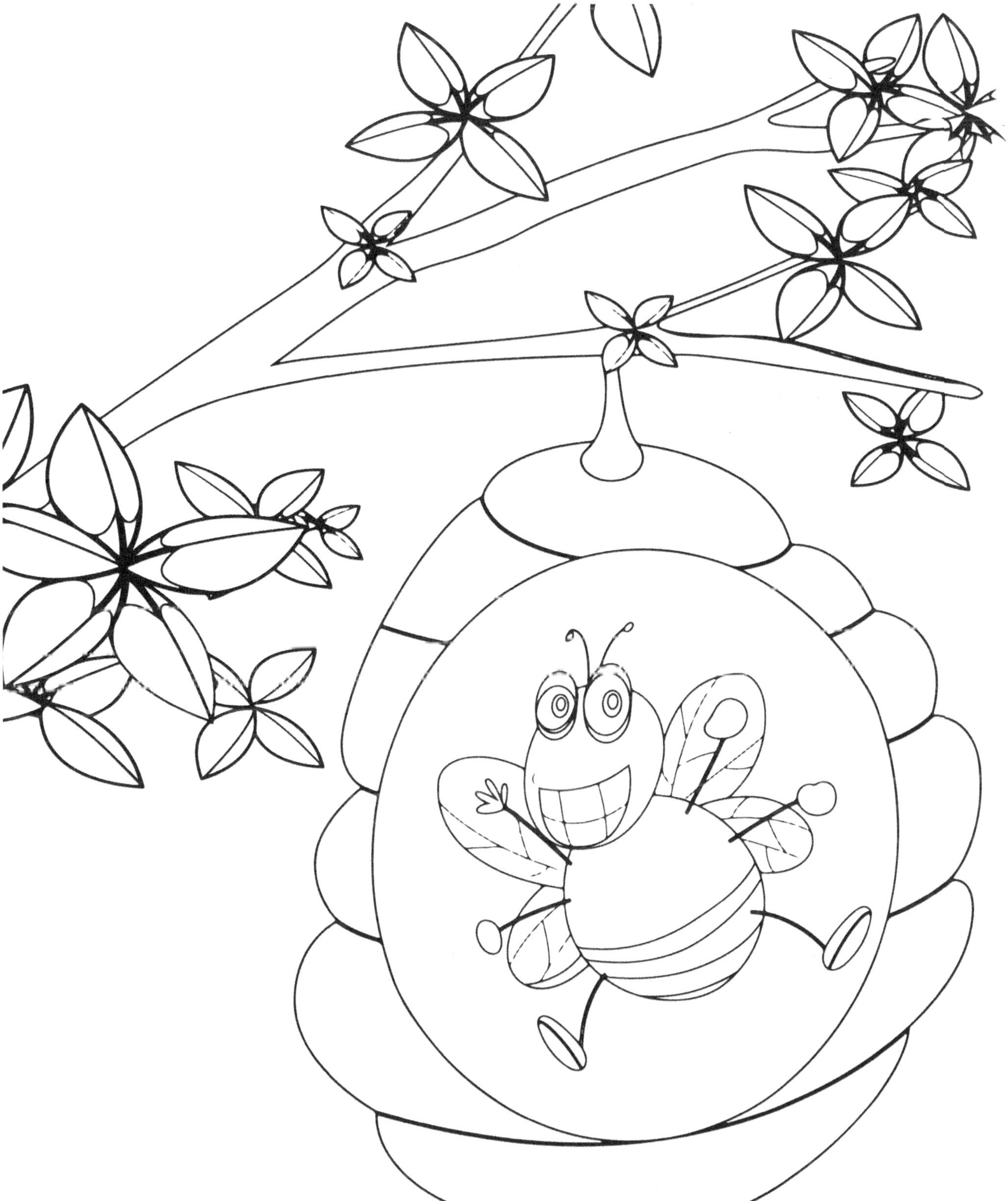

Made in the USA
Middletown, DE
20 February 2023

25260672R00046